D1594356

Delivering WOW

How Dentists Can Build a Fascinating Brand & Achieve More, While Working Less!

Dr. Anissa Holmes

TABLE OF CONTENTS

FOREWORD

Worldwide there are nearly 2 million dentists, and each day we go to work to do two things and only one of those is something we actually learned in school. What did we learn in school? How to practice dentistry. What's the other thing, the one that all those years of school never really prepared us for? How to run a business! And after running a practice for 30 years, I maintain that it is an entirely different animal than the regular small business.

As the publisher of Dentaltown Magazine and the founder of Dentaltown.com, I have been blessed with meeting thousands of dentists. I can't think of one who has grown a practice as quickly and successfully as Dr. Anissa Holmes. She was voted one of the top 25 women in dentistry, and frankly, I think she is one of the top 25 people in dentistry. Period.

The fact is, the business of dentistry is a world unto itself. There are so few quality resources out there for us, which is part of what makes Dr. Holmes' *Delivering WOW: How Dentists Can Build a Fascinating Brand and Achieve More, While Working Less!* such a gem. The vast majority of business books are either a broad overview or a narrowed discussion, which leave you wanting more information, or with the need for five more books on the topics the first didn't bother to address.

Somehow Dr. Holmes has packed everything from social media and branding to team building and ROI — and more — into an easy read. It takes a dentist to know what another dentist would appreciate, and I for one appreciate a book that reads more like fun — while still teaching me a ton — than another pseudo-textbook that makes me want to tear my eyes out.

One of the hardest aspects of the business of dentistry is that being a dentist is a lot like being a satellite. There might be thousands of us up in orbit at the same time, but we are flying solo and doing our best not to crash and burn. Every once in a while though, this great profession of ours is graced with someone who not only has mastered the business of dentistry, but one who chooses to share their experience and their knowledge with the rest of us.

Here's what you're going to find in *Delivering WOW: How Dentists Can Build a Fascinating Brand and Achieve More, While Working Less!* that you're not going to find anywhere else. Dr. Holmes does something that few business authors do, and the fact that she does it as it relates to the business of dentistry is phenomenal. Holmes delivers more than the theoretical foundations and principles of running a good business. She lays out the practical—and even literal—steps for the importance of working not just in their practice, but working on their practice. She is a smart businesswoman and dentist who is doing more than sharing her experience and her success. She is laying out how every dentist can achieve extraordinary results in every facet of their practice.

In the first section of this book you'll be challenged to face whether you have a strong vision for your practice, but more than that, a clear vision for how you approach your business as a whole. Dr. Holmes' clear and concise step-by-step on how to get in there and take action covers everything from developing a thriving company culture, creating everyday systems to keep the business growing, and — my personal favorite — how to establish a brand. Let's not forget that Dr. Holmes is teaching what she's already mastered. After all, she has brilliantly figured out how to master social media with a following of over 50,000 Facebook Fans.

If there's one thing above all else that Dr. Holmes does incredibly well in *Delivering WOW: How Dentists Can Build a Fascinating Brand and Achieve More, While Working Less!*, it's giving the topic of leadership an evidence-based discussion. You are the CEO of your practice and at the forefront of every major decision in and around it, but leadership wasn't a class in dental school, and you're not going to find any CE courses on it either. This is what makes Holmes and her book so invaluable. Page after page, she is able to lay out how to develop leadership skills as a dentist and as a business owner. To do one or the other is impressive enough, but to do both at the same time makes this book worth its weight in gold. The sections on building and maintaining an engaged team are especially eye opening.

Dr. Holmes' passion for helping dentists is something near and dear to my heart. The whole reason I started Dentaltown.com was so that no dentist would ever have to practice alone, and to see this rock star come out with such a solid guide — on top of already giving the dental profession her time as a speaker, podcaster, and clinician — is proof that a dentist can achieve overwhelming success and still have the time and energy to engage her profession in a tremendous way.

I hope you enjoy *Delivering WOW: How Dentists Can Build a Fascinating Brand and Achieve More, While Working Less!* as much as I have.

Howard Farran, DDS, MBA
Founder of Dentaltown.com, and CEO and publisher of Dentaltown Magazine
Bestselling author of *Uncomplicate Business: All It Takes Is People, Time, and Money*

PREFACE

I have been a practicing dentist and an entrepreneur for the past 16 years. In 2011, I walked into my practice and told my team of three that I had a BIG Vision. I wanted to grow. I wanted to make a greater impact on people's lives. I wanted to be different. Perhaps just like you, I had a pretty good business, a supportive team, and very satisfied patients. The problem was I was just going through the motions. I wanted more!

I knew that doing the same old thing would give me the same results. So I hired a coach. I learned the importance of having great mentors and masterminding with people who would hold me accountable. I learned the importance of constant learning and creating an extraordinary customer experience. I learned the significance of knowing my numbers, and the benefits of creating systems so that the business could run without me.

I implemented these business strategies into my dental practice and "WOW!" My team became inspired. My new patient numbers went from 15 to 150. I built a new state-of-the-art office out of profits. I achieved a massive following of over 50,000 Facebook Fans. My practice's revenue increased by 300%! By late 2014, I had reached my goal. I understood the secrets of success. I knew how to "Deliver WOW." Then I set another goal—to share what I had learned to help other dentists around the world to build better practices by Delivering WOW.

I released the Delivering WOW Dental Podcast the first week of 2016 and reached the first page of iTunes New and Noteworthy for Medicine, Education, Business, and Health. Within the first month, the podcast was being listened to in more than 40 countries. I am thrilled to have achieved last year's goal, which was to complete my first book, *Delivering WOW: How Dentists Can Build a Fascinating Brand and Achieve More, While Working Less!*, and am excited about what lies ahead.

ACKNOWLEDGMENTS

Thanks to my parents who always encouraged me to pursue my dreams, and in particular my dad, who taught me from very early the importance of Delivering WOW. Thanks to my husband, Dr. Pierre-John Holmes, for allowing me to experience his beautiful country and for supporting me while I chase all of my big dreams. And finally to Ana and Brady, my beautiful and talented children, who are now checking things off their vision boards and learning to Deliver WOW, thanks for sharing Mom with the world!

INTRODUCTION

Dentists are under increasingly higher stress today. The constant anxiety of paying back student loans, high overheads, and the pressure of running a business are even running some out of the profession altogether.

There must be a better way.

That's why I wrote this book. I wrote this book because I have found a better way. I believe we as dentists can build more profitable and even thriving practices if we take the focus away from doing business as we have always done. This means admitting to ourselves (as well as to our teams) that we do not have all of the answers. This means shifting our mindset and looking carefully at our leadership. This also includes looking at how we build relationships and serve our customers.

Many in our profession, as well as in other small businesses, believe we must work hard for 20 years before we can have the success and freedom we dream of having. They believe in the slow and steady approach.

But that simply does not have to be the case.

After reading this book, you will be able to create a clear vision for your practice and your life, you will better understand what it takes to grow a practice full of "Raving Fans," and you will have created an action plan to guarantee your success. You will be ready to deliver Wow!

If you are a dentist who wants to achieve more by working less and you struggle with building a winning team, growing your new patient numbers, and getting your patients to accept treatment, you're in the right place. If you want to learn how to build a fascinating brand and to use Facebook and other forms of social media to increase the ROI of your marketing campaigns, this book is for you. And if you're tired of feeling guilty, stressed out, and frustrated because you're trying to juggle too much, this book was created specifically to help you!

It's time to create a new reality. Are you ready?

CHAPTER 1

Burnout vs balance

Dr. Scott leans forward and looks into her patient's mouth as she prepares the tooth for a crown. It's a routine procedure Dr. Scott has done many times, but she can practically feel the stress and anxiety radiating from the patient, who, at the last minute, grasps for Dr. Scott's hand to stop her.

"Will it hurt, doctor?" the patient asks, staring intently at Dr. Scott's face.

Dr. Scott gives the patient a reassuring smile. "No, it will not hurt," she says, straightening up and freeing her hand from the patient's grip. Dr. Scott has explained the procedure already but takes the time to do so again as she tries to ease her patient's high anxiety. The patient has a smattering of other questions, all of which were answered earlier in the appointment.

Marie, the receptionist, eases into the tiny room and smiles at the patient, just as Dr. Scott wraps up the explanation. Marie whispers into Dr. Scott's ear. Her heart sinks. The next patient is waiting and is getting restless, even threatening to leave. Dr. Scott takes a quick glance down at her watch. The day has been backed up since the first appointment, where the patient was a late arrival. The appointment after that took longer than it should have, and every appointment since then has started late. And with this patient's high anxiety, Dr. Scott knows this appointment also will run over.

Dr. Scott had hoped to have a lunch break today but knows that will be impossible. She has to see the patient who is waiting, as well as a patient she has agreed to squeeze in for an emergency visit. As Dr. Scott starts to prepare the tooth, she feels her anxiety level rising. She tries to smile politely so the patient will not notice, and even attempts to take in deep breaths to calm her nerves, but it is difficult.

Her lower back is starting to throb and sweat begins to roll slowly down the side of her cheek, as she thinks about the rest of her day. She will not be able to make it to her son's ball game that afternoon, which will cause a fight with her husband when she calls him in between patients to let him know. She missed her son's last ball game as well.

"I can't keep doing this," she thinks, as she can feel her blood pressure climbing higher. The stress of her work is starting to get to her. She had graduated from dental school with such hope and excitement about her new profession, but in the ten years since, something had changed. She no longer feels excited about her work. On too many days, it feels like a grind. She enjoys helping patients, but there is so much more to her job than that. She has a solo practice, and it seems that she has to do everything there. Patient care is a small part of her work when compared to the paperwork, budgeting, and other operational activities.

And when she gets backed up with appointments, as it seems happens more and more these days, nothing seems to go right. Her doctor has just put her on blood pressure medication. Her marriage is under strain, as it appears that she and her husband are always fighting about her work and how it is taking over their lives.

When she wraps up with the patient, she sticks her head into where Marie, the receptionist, sits. "Give me two minutes." She rushes to the restroom and splashes water onto her face, trying to calm her nerves. She stares into the mirror and takes a slow, deep breath. "I can do this."

But as she walks back out to greet her next patient, she wonders if she really can.

Dr. Scott's story is the reality for far too many dentists. Dentistry is a high-stress, high-risk profession where anxiety among patients and their dentists runs high. In fact, research tells us that the incidence of high blood pressure and coronary disease is 25 percent higher among dentists than the general population, and the effects of their work are causing havoc in their lives — their marriages are rocky, their health is in disarray, their happiness is low.

As a practicing dentist, I know just how stressful our work can be. We are taught the ideal of perfection in dental school, and we do our best to attain it. Some might even have every intention to do excellent dentistry, but in fact the dentistry is often rendered imperfect due to time and patient inattention or neglect. Many of us got into this profession because of a desire to help others, but the realities of our work show us that we spend quite a lot of time doing much more than that. We are in small — or even solo — practices where we seem to do all the work. We take care of patients but then stay after to handle bills and budgets, marketing when we can, inventory management, and a host of other activities we didn't anticipate when we were enthusiastic students. We try to take on as many patients as we can — often working during lunch, into the evening, and even on weekends — so we can earn more to take care of the rising overhead costs as well as student loans.

We hope things will improve someday, as we believe we're paying our dues and that it will take time to build our practices. But then we see dentists who have been practicing for more than 20 years, and it seems to us that too many of them are still working as hard as we are, and we then see no end to the constant stress and strain.

This is a recipe for burnout. And it's the reason we see dentists who lose hope and who seem to hate their work. It's also the reason we see some dentists give up on the profession altogether and go off and do something else.

Is that the answer? Is the answer to this high-stress, high-risk work, that we should either hate it or quit it?

I don't believe so.

There is another answer!

This book can be your solution. And that is why I wrote this book. I want to share with you an approach you can use in your practice that can transform the way you work, how you live, and the return on your investment of time, effort, and money, you've put into your studies and your business.

Get your patients to feel the Wow of your practice! The Delivering WOW experience uses innovative approaches and strategies to do just what it promises: deliver Wow. When you use methods and strategies that are focused on giving your patients a Wow experience, you can generate more revenue and create more free time for yourself, so you are no longer crushed under the weight and demand of patient appointments that you must attend to all on your own. With the added revenue you bring in by implementing the Delivering WOW experience, you can build a practice that can run without your day-to-day, constant involvement. You can build the practice you dreamed of when you were a young, hopeful dental student. And you can finally do more of the work of helping people, in a real and sustainable way.

The first mind shift that you must make to fully employ Delivering WOW is that you must see your patients not only as patients, but also as your customers. The reason this shift is so important is that when we think of those we serve as patients, we can get a bit complacent and sometimes feel as if they must come to us because we are the only ones who can help. If a patient has a toothache, he must go to a dentist. He can't go to a dermatologist or an internist. He has to come to us.

But I believe this sense of ... almost entitlement doesn't serve us well, and it doesn't serve our patients well. When you think of your patients as customers, you make a shift from thinking of them as people who must come to you, to thinking of them as people who choose to come to you.

What also starts to happen when you think of your patients as customers is that you can better communicate to find out what they really want. Your patients are not "buying" crowns; they are buying peace of mind that their teeth won't break while on vacation. They are not "buying" scaling and root planning, they are buying peace of mind that their teeth won't get long or loose. When you see patients as individuals who choose to come to you, you begin to consider how you can delight them, so they come back. You want to see how you can deliver Wow.

Treat them as patients, by giving them the dental care they need, but see them as customers whose business you must earn.

Delivering WOW is an approach I first launched in my practice, Jamaica Cosmetic Dental Services, and then began sharing with other dentists and small business owners, so they could implement this concept in their offices. Delivering WOW relies on six essential areas. Those key areas are Vision, Culture, Core Values, Team, Systems, and Brand. When you implement the Delivering WOW experience by giving your practice an overhaul in these critical areas, you will see a remarkable difference in the quality of your practice. While seeing your patients as customers is the first shift, choosing to overhaul each of these key areas is the second shift you must make.

If you make these changes, you will experience massive growth.

CHAPTER 2

Action was my middle name!

My journey as a dentist began when I graduated from the University of Alabama School of Dentistry in 1999. When I got out of dental school, I was ready to take on the world. I was ready to put into practice all that I had learned. I was ready to give back and help others. I was ready to make a difference!

I decided to remain in Birmingham and had the fortunate opportunity to work in several types of practices. One was a very fast-paced, low-fee practice. It was very focused on money. I would often hear the office manager say, "We need to make $10,000 today." I was very uncomfortable in that environment. I knew that money was important, but the core could not be the money. It had to be the people. Relationships. That practice was about high volume and money goals. Needless to say, I left that practice after only six months.

From there, I went to work for a dentist who was really big into cosmetic dentistry and customer service. We did things like bake cookies so that the office would smell like home. We read books like Raving Fans by Ken Blanchard and went to seminars with Dr. Tom Orent. With that opportunity, my eyes were opened and the foundation was laid. After about a year at that practice, I opened my own office, which focused on providing excellent care and great service.

I enjoyed beautifying people's smiles and changing lives. I set up the waiting area like a living room and served coffee, tea, and baked cookies. From the very beginning, I thought about ways to create uniqueness and at the same time be profitable.

I did a little research and discovered that there weren't

many dentists who were providers for kids with Medicaid in Birmingham. I saw this as an opportunity to grow my practice as well as to serve those who many were not willing to serve. I dedicated one full day to treating these incredible kids. We also set up an alliance with a local pediatric dentist, who referred all of their teenage patients to us. About half of the patients were foster kids who were brought in with their social workers. It felt really great to give these kids a great experience and make them our VIPs.

We were one of the few dental offices where teenagers with Medicaid could get their wisdom teeth removed. My husband, an oral surgery resident at the time, would come in on Saturdays to treat them. We received so much love from these children, and they changed our lives.

Being one of the few offices in Birmingham to see kids with Medicaid, this also became a huge profit center for the practice.

Another area of creating uniqueness was in identifying that there were many Spanish-speaking immigrants to our area. We realized that no dental office focused on serving these patients. One of my hygienists, Mayra, was a dentist who had trained in Mexico. She did not have a U.S. dental degree, so she was not able to practice dentistry in Alabama. Upon joining the office, I sent her to receive her dental hygiene training and license. One day Mayra came to me with a brilliant idea!

She recommended that we place an ad in the local Spanish newspaper. She said that there were so many Spanish-speaking members of the community, but there was no dental office that focused on treating them. She said that it could be very frustrating for them not to be able to communicate with their doctor, and she wanted to help them. Eventually both of my front desk employees, and in fact, everyone in the office spoke Spanish. I even took classes and learned to speak Spanish to better communicate with these patients. We saw a need and we filled it. These patients were so grateful to find a dental office where the team could communicate effectively with them. They, in turn, became "raving fans," and spread the word about our practice.

As I had done with the patients who had Medicaid, I was willing to serve an underserved market. I served people who may have been overlooked by other providers. As a result of doing something different, we were very profitable from very early on.

In 2005, my husband and I decided to move to Jamaica. My husband, an oral and maxillofacial surgeon, grew up in Jamaica. With only one or two oral surgeons on the island, he knew that Jamaica would be where he could make the greatest impact. My commitment was that when I moved to Jamaica nothing would change. My practice would be the same as if it was in the States. I knew that with a quick 1-hour flight I would be able to get back stateside for continuing education and that I would have easy access to the same dental suppliers and labs that I used when my practice was in Birmingham.

I started working in Jamaica as an independent contractor in a well-established practice to learn the business culture of Jamaica. After five years, my husband and I realized that we would make Jamaica our permanent home, so I decided to start a new practice, Jamaica Cosmetic Dental Services. I started this practice in an 800-square foot space with only three operatories.

After two years, I walked into the practice and announced to my team that we were moving. They said, "Dr. Holmes, we just moved to this office."

My response was, "I know, but I have a BIG vision."

At that same time, I decided to get a business coach to help me to achieve my vision, to be the top dental practice in the country known for Delivering WOW.

Up until that "aha" moment, we were on a traditional slow and steady growth path for a dental office. I struggled with managing cash flow. I knew there were certain areas I needed to put money to grow the business. Unfortunately, I always had to balance what needed to be purchased, with having cash in the bank.

A year later, we doubled our revenue and tripled our capacity to a 2,500-square foot space. When building the new location, I made the decision not to borrow money. Perhaps I could have grown faster if I had borrowed, but that's not the path I wanted to take. I accepted that things would be tight. Profits would be reinvested into the business to buy equipment. I made personal sacrifices to hold off on spending, so I could put that money into the company.

Before I decided to get a coach, I was a typical dentist, feeling that if I provided high-quality dentistry and gave good service, my database of customers would grow. And while I saw some growth, I knew there was more I could do in that area. Once introduced to coaching, I started to dissect the business. I began to look at how I was running it and realized the traditional, slow-growth approach that many dentists were taking just wasn't going to work for me. I wanted to build a great business to enjoy now, not wait a dozen more years.

I realized that if I had one good growth strategy and it was working, that was great. But if I had multiple strategies that were working, that would be the fuel I needed to multiply my business. Studying and coming up with strategies eventually led to Delivering WOW, which I am describing in this book.

Since focusing on building our culture, systems, and brand, the growth of the business has been phenomenal. As I write this chapter, for instance, just last month we had more than 250 new patients. That's a number a lot of practices would dream of having over several months or even a year. And we got that number in just one month. In another example of our growth, our marketing budget was $500. We saw a return of $8,000. That's a 1,500 percent return on our investment! In yet another instance, we implemented one new system that increased our revenue by $20,000 a month. All of these are typical examples of what can happen when you begin to deliver Wow. I will share the exact steps of how I produced those numbers later in this book, but I wanted to share my experience as you start to think of your own practice.

The time freedom and the ability to give — even the ability to give away dental services to needy members of my community — are all benefits I mainly attribute to Delivering WOW. Before, I was like many of the dentists I know, in that I was working way too many hours and feeling the pressure of increasing overhead costs. However, I was not okay with that. I knew there must be a better way.

From very early I knew that I wanted to be a doctor. While in college, I had an excellent opportunity to attend a summer program at the dental school at the University of Alabama. As part of that program, I was able to spend the summer working in the pediatric dental clinic. I met an amazing resident, Dr. Sanchez, who shared with me her passion for treating kids and for dentistry. She also shared that dentistry was a great profession, as it offered a lot of flexibility to have a balanced life. She also talked a lot about the ability to make a difference and give back to the community.

The aspect of helping others has always been important to me. I did lots of community service in high school and while in dental school, I went to Central America and did mission work. My chosen profession seemed a perfect fit.

However, once running my practice, as with most dentists, I found that my income wasn't what I wanted, and I didn't always have the time to help others in the way I dreamed. Yes, I created beautiful smiles and helped patients reduce or eliminate their fear. But I focused too much time working in and not on the business.

Delivering WOW has helped me to change all that. I now have a dedicated and fantastic team, and together we deliver Wow to patients day in and day out. The practice has grown significantly over the past couple of years since adopting this new approach. As a result of this growth, we have had to hire additional hygienists and dentists. In addition to the increase in revenue, one of the real results of this change is the fact that I now have much more free time than I did before — time to spend with my family, connect with friends, or invest in other activities of my choosing. My practice can run well whether I am in the office or away.

So what exactly is Delivering WOW? Well, that's what thc next chapter answers ...

DELIVERING WOW ACTION ACTIVITY

Take an honest look at your life today. Are you happy? How has your practice affected your personal life? Write down just what kind of impact your practice has on your life and what you would like to change.

CHAPTER 3

What is Delivering WOW?

Are you tired of doing the same old things and getting the same results? Do you want to have more freedom? Do you wish to know the secret to success? Well, it all starts with Delivering WOW.

Delivering WOW means that your ultimate vision is to create a practice that can run without you. This doesn't mean that you will stop practicing dentistry, although some who achieve this level of success choose to do so. It means that your practice is so efficient that if you were to decide to take a vacation for six months, your team and systems could run your practice. It means that you go to work because you want to, and not because you have to. It means that your patients have peace of mind because the dentistry that you provide is meticulous, beautiful, and long-lasting. It means that you have a unique culture known for providing extraordinary experiences even for the most fearful patients and that your patients grow your business for you. Does this seem like a dream? Well, listen up, because it can be your reality.

Delivering WOW is a customer-focused results-oriented approach that service businesses, including dental practices, can use to provide a consistently high level of service and excellence. Delivering WOW focuses on building relationships and taking action in six core areas, and can revolutionize how you run your business. It is important that you take the time to master each step, as they build upon each other. For example, no great business owner has built a remarkable brand without first having a vision for their company.

Delivering WOW can quickly transform a struggling,

cash-strapped practice into a dynamic practice that experiences massive growth, and can turn an ordinary practice into the leading dental office in the community. The reason this approach works is because it focuses on specific areas that affect the business's relationship with its customers: Vision, Culture, Core Values, Team, Systems, and Brand.

I will provide specific details for each step in the Delivering WOW experience later, but let me tell you why each area is so important. This book will help you to understand the importance of working on each of these areas if you want to provide Wow experiences for your patients and achieve more for your life.

Vision is the first step of the Delivering WOW experience and is perhaps the most important. Your vision is your BIG dream for your practice. Your vision as a dentist will affect your entire practice, as well as your future growth. Your vision will also influence the speed at which you will achieve your personal dreams. If you do not have a vision, then anything can happen, because there is no detailed roadmap of how you will achieve your goals. Your vision is the big idea you have for your business, and ultimately, your life.

Culture is the next step of the Delivering WOW experience and is important because it is the story that you want to tell about your practice. It is what you want to be known for. Every practice has a culture, whether you create it, or it evolves. Being focused on your company culture helps ensure that you are developing the environment to bring forth your vision.

The next step in the Delivering WOW experience is creating your core values. Your core values are the rules of your company. They declare what your practice stands for, and are used when making all of the decisions for your practice. Core values are also important because they help you live out your culture, and they are critical to achieving your vision. For example, if one of your core values is "pursue growth and learning," and a team member continuously refuses to attend continuing education courses, they would be operating outside of your core values and would not be a good fit for your practice.

Once you have clearly defined your vision, culture, and core values, the next step is to align your team. Some of you already have a great team, who can help you develop the core values for your practice. Others may realize that some shifts may have to be made to the current team.

The key point here is that all members of your team must be aligned with the practice's vision for it to be achieved. It can't be your vision alone; it has to be the vision of everyone in your practice. It's also vital for your team to have personal visions for themselves, and know that through working in your practice, they can achieve all of their personal dreams.

Once you know where you are headed and you have the right team, the next step is to look at your systems. Systems are essential for scaling up your operation. If you are stuck and feel as if you have to do every single thing in your practice, then it's because you do not have the proper systems in place. If you're providing inconsistent experiences to patients, this is also a weakness that is showing up because of lack of adequate systems. If you want consistency in your practice, or if you wish to create a practice that can run without you, then you must have written systems.

The next step of the Delivering WOW experience is in developing a fascinating brand. A brand is a result of all of the earlier crucial areas working together. Your brand is what people say about you when you are not around — it is not about your logo, it's about how people feel when they describe your company. It's what attracts your ideal patients. Creating a fascinating brand will separate you from the next dental practice in the mind of your patients. Internal and external marketing are great ways to share your brand and let the world know all of the fascinating things that you are doing. This book will also focus on these critical areas.

By the way, can you guess what is the ultimate goal of the Delivering WOW experience? Yes, it's achieving your vision.

Delivering WOW is about helping you to build a fascinating brand. It's about getting more done in less time. It's about positioning your business as something unique within your community. Take our practice, for example. Our vision is to be the leading dental practice in Jamaica known for Delivering WOW.

Our work in the area of Wow experiences has positioned us in the community as a dental office that is very different. The same can be for your practice, no matter where you are located. What Wow means for your practice may be different than what Wow means for mine. But the common thread is that Wow will be about exceptional service and superior care. From the moment a patient enters our office, our goal is to Wow them. The patient is welcomed with a smile, offered a beverage such as hot chocolate, gourmet tea, or Café Blue coffee — among Jamaica's finest coffees — and invited to enjoy a freshly baked plantain tart.

We know some patients experience anxiety when they visit a dentist, so we provide iPads to take away the sound, as well as hand and arm massages to take away tension and to relax their minds. We offer toothbrushes in the restroom so patients can brush, and we offer scented lotions and perfumes so they can feel at home.

These amenities are what make up the Wow experience that customers see, but there is so much more to Delivering WOW in our office. Medical offices are notorious for being off-schedule. It's not uncommon for patients to wait for exceptionally long times before being seen.

We realize this and want our patients to know we value their time. In fact, we offer an on-time guarantee. If a patient is not seated within 15 minutes of his or her appointment time, the next exam is free.

These are just some of the offerings we have put in place to set our practice apart and to Wow our customers. And it works! We regularly get 5-star ratings and feedback from customers commenting on the special way in which they were treated. This translates to more word-of-mouth and more customers.

That's what Wowing customers looks like in our office. In your office, it might be something different. But whatever it is, it needs to be something unique that goes beyond what others are doing. That's the true nature of Delivering WOW.

It's about truly being a cut above. It's about being unique. It's about being different.

You may be wondering how is it possible to add so many amenities or do something like providing an on-time guarantee in a dental practice. Well, that's what the next several chapters will explain. The next chapters will describe in detail the six core areas, so you see how each fits into the overall Wow experience and helps you to do what you need to do to stand out.

Are you ready? Let's get to it!

DELIVERING WOW ACTION ACTIVITY

Evaluate your readiness for making fundamental changes in your practice. Are you willing to change the way you operate? Are you ready to do the hard work of putting in place certain actions, systems, and processes to overhaul your practice? Why or why not?

CHAPTER 4

Vision

What is your vision? What is that one big goal that you want to achieve for your life? Have you clearly defined it? Is it written down?

As dentists, many of us just go to work day in and day out, and before we realize it years have passed, but we are in the same place. We still haven't taken that European vacation, we still haven't paid off our credit cards, and we still are not spending enough time with those who matter most. So what happened? Well, we didn't plan; I mean really plan for success. It was more like "At some point I will ..." vs. setting goals with a roadmap of how we would get there. The reason that I discuss personal vision first is that for most of us, our practice will provide the income for us to achieve our personal dreams.

I went through life for many years knowing that I wanted to be successful. But that was it. I didn't define exactly what success was. I was not specific about what success would look like. I wasn't taking steps to reach specific goals. I thought that if I was serving my community, and I was making my patients happy, then I would have a successful practice. However, once I set a clearly defined vision with an extremely specific goal, I was able to achieve so much more, and in less time. I now even have a vision board that shows in picture form, what I want for my life. This vision board has photos of places that I would like to travel and experiences that I would like to have with my family.

Regarding my practice, my vision was very specific, and it's what I shared with you in an earlier chapter: To be the leading dental practice in Jamaica known for Delivering WOW. I had to look at that vision and then determine how I would get there.

Once you create your personal vision, it's time to create one for your business.

As you evolve as a practice leader, you must learn to think more strategically and clearly. If your vision is to be successful, then make sure to define success. What do you want to achieve in one year, in five, or perhaps when you retire? Not only write down what you want but paint a clear picture of your vision in your mind and see yourself achieving it. Visualize your success. If you can dream it, you can achieve it!

So how can you go from a vague idea of being successful, to living out your vision?

1. **Clearly define your vision.** It isn't enough to simply say that you want to be successful. You must be specific. Visualizing what you intend to achieve will help you know what you are working toward, as well as will help you determine priorities.

2. **Write down your vision.** When you are setting your vision, it's important to write it down. Writing down your vision helps to take it from your head and put it in a tangible form you can see and feel. That's exactly what happened to me.

3. **See it in picture form.** Creating a vision board will allow you to activate yourself in a way that merely seeing the vision written down in words alone cannot. Doing the exercise of creating a vision board will help you to engage your senses and to focus your mind on the task in front of you.

4. **Create your plan.** What do you need to do to ensure that you achieve your goal? For us to become the leading dental practice in Jamaica, we had to build a new office. We had to determine what would be unique about the practice to make us stand out. We had to create specific systems and practices that would

encourage a consistent delivery of a Wow experience.

5. **Act on the plan.** Be very specific about the goals that you would like to achieve, who will help you to achieve them, and set a deadline of when they must be accomplished. Make sure to write down which action items must be checked off daily, weekly, or monthly until your goal is achieved. Each of these steps is significant in going from merely wishing and wanting something, to creating a clear vision, and then to actually making it happen.

A vision without action is just passing time. Your business is not finished its growth and development until your vision becomes a reality. From there, your vision will grow, and you can then set new goals for your business. Not only do you need to create a personal vision and vision for your practice, but you also need to inspire your team to create personal visions for themselves. They need to see how being a part of the practice's vision can help them achieve their personal goals.

Get to your why

Do you want more time, money, or freedom? Exploring your why will help define your priorities, aspirations, and in turn, your vision. When it comes to the vision you have for your life and your practice, take the time to clearly define what you want to achieve. If you are having trouble determining your vision, start with your "why." Why is reaching this goal important to you? What will achieving this goal provide for you? Once you know what you are working for, then you naturally become very excited about seeing it come to life. My big why to achieving my personal vision is that I want the freedom to travel the world with my family; I want to leave a legacy for my future generations. I want that when I celebrate my 80th birthday people will share stories of how I impacted their lives. Once I got to my why it was easy to create my vision. Next, I had to take action steps to achieve it.

Unfortunately, many people do not look ahead. They are going to work day after day earning an income, and that's it. That's all they see for themselves. There is no vision there. However, you don't have to be one of those people. Once you have a clear picture of why you are working, your life begins to have more purpose. Once you have a vision of what you want, you find a way, whether it's through reading more books, having a coach help you to fast-track your success, getting more training, or joining a mastermind.

Life is about balance!

Having a balanced life is about being able to be fulfilled, not just through your business, but having a fulfilled life where you are living without regret. For me, it's spending time with my family and friends. Exercising. Being healthy.

Some people are putting way too much time into the business that they have no time left for the other areas of their lives. They aren't putting the time and effort into growing their marriages, so their marriages are suffering. They neglect their health, so they see illnesses and conditions that come as result of this neglect. They aren't giving their children time, so there are regrets once their kids are all grown up and they realize that they never took the time to have great conversations or they missed critical events.

Indeed creating a vision for your life helps you to assess just where you are and what you need to change. Your business is not your whole life. It's just one part of your life. It's a vehicle to help you achieve your personal dreams. Your business is what gives you the freedom to spend more time on what matters most, not take you away from those things.

More strategies for success: The success wheel

When looking at life, there are so many daily and weekly tasks that you can use to fill your time. I like to see life as a pie, with many different slices that make it complete. Every slice is vital to capturing the full essence of the pie —your life.

Some of the slices of the pie of life are time at work, time with a spouse, time with kids, time with friends, time to exercise, personal development, spiritual time, meditation, and giving back to the community.

Here is the success wheel. You can download a copy of the success wheel at www.deliveringwow.com/successwheel

Do you find that your life is unbalanced? Are there areas where you know you need to spend more time? Even if you find that you are happy, overall, there may still be one or two areas you want to work on.

If your child were chosen to be the lead in a school play or chosen for an elite sports group, you would probably find a way to get them to the activity. However, we, as adults often say we are too busy to do things that give us happiness or better health. The thing is, there is never enough time to do everything, but there is always time to do what matters most.

One tool you can use to ensure that you accomplish what matters most is to create a default diary. A default diary is a plan where you schedule important tasks at set times, so they get done. The idea is that we're often so busy doing low-priority or urgent tasks that we never get around to doing what is necessary and beneficial to our long-term growth. So the default diary sets a predetermined time for doing these important activities.

I found that I was working so much that I didn't spend time with friends. So in my default diary, I set aside time every Wednesday night to spend time with friends, whether that was dinner or some other activity. I also set aside time during the week from 5-7 p.m., where I would focus on spending time with the kids.

Visit www.deliveringwow.com/defaultdiary for a template to create your default diary. With this default diary, you can schedule patient treatment time, time to work on your business, and all of the other things that are most important, such as exercise, date night, and time with your family. Do not let anything encroach on these non-negotiables, as they are what you have defined as what matters most.

Also, have your team create their personal diaries, mapping out what they will accomplish in the workday as well as in their personal lives.

When you use a default diary to help implement your vision, you find that there is time to do everything you want to do. A lot of people say, "I don't have time," but it's because they are spending time on what doesn't matter.

This one tip of using a default diary can transform

the way you work and live. So if you set a vision but feel that you have no way of achieving it because you feel you don't have the time, then consider this tip. A default diary can help you get to your vision, and it can help you avoid many of the traps others in our profession experience — burnout, poor relationships, and poor health.

Break your vision down into stages

Once we set our big goal to be the leading practice known for Delivering WOW, we knew that the next step was to take action. We put in place a passionate team. We overhauled our entire office, picking apart and implementing new procedures, training our team on various aspects of the Wow experience, and more.

It's important to break down your vision into stages. If you simply approach your vision as that big, final attainment, it can be difficult to know how to get there. But if you break it down into stages, let's say you break it down into years, then it can be a lot easier to manage, and it can be a lot more likely that you will realize that vision.

For instance, in my case, I plan my next year the December before. From there, I break my goals down by quarters, by months, and then weeks. This helps me know what to do and what to focus on at any given time. I look at 15 things I want to happen that quarter and then plan it. Of course, this doesn't mean I must personally do each of these things. My team does many of these tasks. We will discuss team a bit later in this book, but your team can be your number one asset.

If you are setting a vision and you want to be in a

particular place in five years, then determine where you need to be in three years, and then where you need to be in one year. From there, break it down even more. Be sure to set a vision for your personal life as well as your business, as the two are intertwined.

When you plan in this way, don't be discouraged if a life event happens to throw you off the plan a little. Life happens. Sometimes you plan for a particular event or activity to happen in one month, but it can't happen that month because of the life event. That's OK. Don't let your plans stall because not everything falls perfectly just the way you had it on the schedule. Just be flexible and shift that activity to the next month where it can happen. Do the best you can.

When you plan in this way, you can look back on the year and realize just how much you've accomplished, because you took the time to break down big goals into small goals. If you follow this system, don't be surprised if you achieve more goals and in a shorter time than you planned.

Create vision and mission statements

Once you have developed your vision for your business, it is helpful to create a vision statement as well as a mission statement to govern your office. Your vision statement speaks to the aspirations of the company. What is the vision you have for the company and how will it affect the lives of your patients, the community, or others? Your vision statement is aspirational. Your vision statement is something that is big, and that inspires others. It's the big thing you are working toward. Write this out in a succinct, clear sentence.

Your mission statement helps you focus on that big idea. The mission statement takes its cue from your vision. The mission statement should be clear and specific. A vision is the overall destination — where you are going. A mission is why you exist. Think of the vision as the future state you hope to attain, while the mission addresses the current state you are in, and the work you are doing now to get to that vision.

Inspire your team's vision

It's important to engage those in your vision who will play a significant role in helping you to accomplish it. In the case of a dental practice, this includes your team. Be sure to help your team see how your overall vision for the business will help them to accomplish their goals. I often speak of vision at our office, and my team is just as excited about it as I am. That is because it is a shared vision by now. We all want to have the best dental practice in the country. I have helped my team see how being the best dental practice in the country will impact each of their lives. They understand that once the business is profitable, they can earn greater compensation as I share the increasing profits with them. This increasing compensation enables them to do the things in their lives to achieve their personal dreams.

When you think big, and you write down what you want and focus on what matters most, you achieve your goals.

Once you start to look at your vision, you begin to dream. Your thinking will expand, and you will be able to achieve things you never thought possible. Your vision will evolve as you grow, just as mine did. This is the power of vision.

DELIVERING WOW ACTION ACTIVITY

Take the time to write down your vision for your life. Make a list of all of the activities you do that make you happy. Next, make a list of all of the activities you do every day. Now compare the two lists. Do you need to make a shift?

Then from there, focus on and write down the vision for your practice.

•

Talk to your team about your vision for the practice and how the practice can help them to achieve their personal dreams. Then have them create vision boards by cutting and pasting pictures of places they would like to go, experiences they would like to have, and things they would like to purchase. Take a group photo and place it on your social media pages, such as Facebook, Instagram, Twitter, and Google Plus. Display this in your office and share in your new patient office tours.

On a scale of 1-10 with 10 being the happiest, write down how happy you are in each area of your life. Next, write down beside your current number where you want to be in one year. This exercise will show you where you must focus.

CHAPTER 5

Culture

We grew up with a myth! This myth is that to be successful, we must be better than everyone else. We must try harder and work longer. We must be better in school, be better than our teammates, and be better than other applicants. We have been conditioned to copy what others are doing, and then try to do that same thing better.

The reality, however, is that what is better than being better, is being unique.

While businesses have put a lot of focus on being "better," customers are focusing on something entirely different. They are focusing on getting the best deal. They are looking at all of the options that are the same, and choosing the cheapest option.

When you can successfully differentiate yourself, however, you become the go-to person or company for one particular reason. That is when you can charge higher fees. That is when you can dominate your market. What is better than being "better" is being different.

One of the first steps to standing out and being different is in the story that you want to tell about your practice: Your culture.

In building a dynamic dental practice, culture has to be top-of-mind when you are planning the transformation of your business. Once you create your culture, you will attract team members and patients who are aligned with or who can identify with that culture. They feel an emotional connection with your business.

To build a fascinating brand, start with your culture. Leading brands clearly point out their differences.

These differences can be small, but they must be clearly defined. The fact is, people can replicate your services, your systems can be beaten, people can outdo your strengths, but nobody can copy who you are.

Decide what will be unique about your practice. Will it be a phenomenal patient experience, an on-time guarantee, or will it be additional services that other offices in your community are not providing? Think about the experience you have when you go to Starbucks. It's more than just the coffee that draws people in. People have an emotional connection. It's the aroma; it's how the baristas make you feel.

Culture can mean different things to different dental practices. For us, it's about VIP amenities and treating every patient like family. It's about the way we make patients feel by providing iPads and Bluetooth headphones to take away the sound, or complimentary arm and hand massages to relax patients before their dental visit. We have put a lot of thought into our culture and how we can be unique. We even have a coffee table culture book in our reception area for patients to see photos of us having fun behind the scenes or out building stronger communities.

When building our culture, it was important for us to find out what our patients wanted, what mattered most, so we could focus on it. So we asked them! We asked patients while in our office, polled our Facebook Fans, and sent out surveys to patients the day after their appointments asking how we could serve them better. We found out that there were different priorities for different patients, but the answers were consistent. Our patients wanted three things:

1.) **To be seen on time.** Some of our patients are busy. They don't have a lot of time. What mattered most for them was being seen on time, or being given a phone call if we knew we would be running behind schedule.

2.) **To have quality and consistency of their dental services.** They wanted their dental work to be beautiful, look natural, and be long-lasting. They wanted "peace of mind."

3.) **To have a great experience.** Many patients have had bad experiences, and are extremely fearful when going to the dentist. What mattered most to them was finding a dental home that could take care of their dental concerns with little to no pain.

Once we found out what mattered most, we built our culture around that. Our coffee and tea bar includes gourmet Blue Mountain coffee, specialty teas, hot chocolate, and freshly baked plantain tarts. Our bathrooms have toothbrushes, scented lotions, and perfumes. Our patients finish their visit with a warm peppermint scented towel.

We also implemented an on-time guarantee. If patients are not seen within 15 minutes of their appointment time, their next exam is free. To make this happen, we had to have the right team in place to carry patients to the treatment area on time and to start with the office tour, X-rays, patient education videos, and the hand massages.

We also call patients when we know we are running behind to adjust the time they should arrive. The patients appreciate this courtesy, as they know that we value their time.

One of the other essential elements of our culture is our team. We invest in our team, and it shows. We constantly praise our team, be it face-to-face, in front of patients, or on social media. My team recently attended a dental conference, and they felt like celebrities because teams from other offices kept coming up to them and calling them by name!

One of my team members shared a story that in the office where she used to work, employees always had to look like they were busy, even if there was "nothing to do." And the lunch hour was strictly adhered to; employees had to be sure to eat and get back to work within that time. That's not our culture. If you're hungry, and there is no patient, it's OK to get a cup of tea. Our practice is not a place where team members have to pretend to be busy or suffer hunger pains simply because of the clock on the wall. Our team takes care of our patients, and we take care of our team. Our team works through lunch or stays late to get the job done. That's the culture we have.

We used to have to go and look for people to hire, but because of our company culture, we no longer have to look for people to hire. Now, we have individuals who work for other dentists, calling us because they know about our culture. They call to ask, "What do I have to do to be a part of your team?"

We are also known for being charitable. We have given away smile makeovers, and built a playground and computer lab for a school. We donate proceeds from new patient exams to a different charity every month. In giving, we receive. Building communities is part of our story.

What story are you telling?
What culture will you create?

By the way, culture isn't just about what your customers see. While culture ultimately shows up in what your customers see, it starts inside. Culture begins with what is going on in your practice. Culture is made up of how you treat your employees, how they treat each other, and how your office functions. If your team is unhappy, or there is a lot of backbiting or drama, then that will spill over into the experience your customers have. You can't have a negative internal company culture and present a positive customer experience. It just doesn't happen.

Every company has a culture, whether it was designed, or it evolved. We have all been to a business where the employees were rude or it looked like they were doing us a favor. The facility was not clean, the service was subpar, and the quality of the product was nothing special. Maybe it was a restaurant. Maybe it was a clothing store. Maybe it was a dental office. These businesses clearly have a culture that has evolved. Either the business owner is absent or hasn't taken the time to think about the story that it wants to tell. As a result, things "just happen." You don't want things just to happen in your practice.

A default culture will never contribute to a Wow experience for your customer.

Building a great culture starts at the top. It begins with you as the leader. Decide what you want to be known for and enlist your team to help you create and share your story.

So how do you do that? Well, in addition to making sure you are treating employees with respect, it's also important to make sure you provide the tools they need to succeed in your office. I will discuss this more in the team chapter, but does everyone know his or her job description? Does everyone have the right resources to do the tasks you have assigned? Do employees feel as if their opinions matter and that they are heard when they have something to say? All of this contributes to the environment and culture you create.

As your business grows, the importance of culture grows. That is because the culture can be a significant factor in just how your company moves forward. Culture affects not only the types of customers you attract, but also the kinds of employees you attract. If you want the best employees, then you'll need to make sure you are providing the best work environment. This isn't necessarily about putting in a lot of the amenities we see in some places like Silicon Valley and tech companies. Amenities like game rooms, catered meals, and the like. No, this is about creating an environment of open communication, functional operations, and an investment in the professional development of your employees.

At our office, we have instituted weekly lunch and learns, where we work on systems, discuss a book we are all reading, or do some other activity that is focused on helping the team learn together. That spirit of learning started with me, because as the leader of the practice, I had first to be the example.

I turned my car into a driving university, where I listen to books on Audible or podcasts while commuting. I even listen while working out. The learning doesn't stop at the office because now we have a culture of learning there also.

Instituting the lunch and learns, purchasing Kindles for the team, and setting aside time for team development is an investment I am happy to make because I know it will pay off personally for my team, as well as for the company.

The importance of culture in achieving your vision

Once you have built a fascinating company culture that consistently exceeds patients' expectations and have the right team who are in line with the company culture, your vision will be easy to achieve. Your patients will become "raving fans" and won't stop sharing stories about their experiences in your office. Your culture, once done right, builds your brand, which gets you one step closer to achieving your vision.

DELIVERING WOW ACTION ACTIVITY

Evaluate the current culture of your practice. What is unique about your practice? What story do you want to tell? Conduct a brainstorming session with your team on what you can do to be different from other dental practices in your community and list action items you will implement each month over the next 12 months to continue to build your culture.

CHAPTER 6

Core values

Now that you know the type of vision you are working toward and the culture that will help you get there, it's time to look at the core values necessary for creating that culture.

Core values are the rules of the game. They define what your practice stands for and how you will achieve your vision. If you focus on the wrong core values, you could end up with the wrong culture, a company culture that is not attractive to your ideal customer, nor those you prefer to hire. This chapter not only explores the importance of core values but also gives strategies for how to make sure your company is establishing the right core values for the business you are building and growing.

Why are core values essential to a dental practice?

Core values help form the culture of your practice and help enable you to reach your vision. Core values guide all of the decisions you make for your practice. For instance, if one of your core values is "Use the highest quality materials," then any materials that are not of the highest quality are eliminated. If one of your core values is to "Hire and develop the best," then you will always ensure that you are hiring the top people for your practice. If one of your core values is "Customer obsession," then you will be a fanatic about over-delivering in the area of customer service. If you have a team member who is rude to a patient, that would go against the core values of the practice, and might be a reason for the team member to be let go.

If you are not clear about your core values, then you will find that you are always making decisions based on changing values or ideas. One month, you may make a purchase because it is the cheapest option. In another month, you may make a purchase because you found the highest quality option. Those two decisions are based on two different core values. Running an office in this way is likely to produce frustration and a chaotic operation. Knowing and sticking to your core values makes the office run more smoothly.

Another reason why core values are essential to your practice is that they can become a calling card for you. When you share your core values with the public, then these core values let your customers know just whom it is they are dealing with, and what to expect. For instance, if one of your core values is to "Value patient feedback," then your patient has a reasonable expectation that you may be more likely to hear her out when she expresses concern or disappointment, than another dental practice that does not have that as a core value.

Need for choosing the right core values

Be careful when identifying your core values. Don't choose core values simply because they sound good or will look good on a plaque on the wall of your waiting area. Be deliberate. Choose core values that are right for your practice. That is because you must be able to live up to your core values. You must live them, and they become a part of you. So when you are doing something fascinating in your practice, it will always be linked back to one of your core values. Your core values are an essential element to defining and building your brand.

Your core values are the heartbeat of your practice. They are about who you are as a practice, and what you hold dear. They are about how you relate to team members and how you relate to patients and others outside of your practice.

We all have personal values. So how do you determine those that are the core values of your practice? One way is to get your team involved. It can be helpful to bring in key members of your team and discuss core values. Remember, I said core values must be true to you — they must be authentic. So don't just make them up or write them down because they seem nice. Identify the values that are already present within your practice. Focus on those values that support your vision.

Write down all of the values for your practice and create a list. Does this list seem like the right fit for your practice? Can these core values stand the test of time? Or will they need to change in a month, six months, or a year? As you read over your list of core values, be sure they resonate with who you are as the leader of your practice and what you see your practice becoming.

If these values seem to support your vision, they can become a framework for your culture.

Show off your core values

Your core values should not be a secret! Share them with your patients and the community! Along with your company's vision and mission statements, print and display your core values. Place them in a prominent spot in the office. Point them out to new patients during your office tour. Once your team members are in line with the company's core values, they will strive to give you and your patients their absolute best.

Enlist your team to build your core values

Very early in the transformation to a Delivering WOW practice, we were working on culture, and I sat down with the team and asked, "What's important to us? How do we want to be known in the community?"

I could have done this on my own, but it would not have been nearly as powerful as involving my team. Getting my employees involved gave them a sense of ownership of the process. In considering what we wanted to be known for, we listed several things.

These are the core values that spoke to the culture of our business:

• Always show compassion. It's important to truly understand our patients' needs and meet them there. We want to treat our patients with kindness and understanding.

• Ask the right questions. It's important for us to be able to listen to understand. Understanding our patients' fears, concerns, and points of resistance helps us to treat them properly and provide better solutions to their problems.

• Deliver a Wow experience every time. Consistency is important.

• Listen with two ears and one heart. The heart in business had to be compassion, love, and understanding.

• Pursue growth and learning. We have weekly lunch and learn sessions to ensure we are always learning as a team. All of our team members also have Kindles to read books to help with their personal development.

• Think big and have fun. We are innovative and think outside of the box. We have a relaxed working environment where we love going to work, and the patients feel it.

• Build a positive team and family spirit. If we aren't working together as a team, then we can't serve our patients to the best of our ability.

• Insist on the highest standards. We want the best for our patients regarding the quality of dentistry that we provide as well as the environment in which we provide it.

• Build a stronger community. We will always make giving back to the community a part of our culture.

• Be humble. As we grow, we want always to remain grateful for what we have and humble in how we carry ourselves.

One of our core values mentioned above is "Pursue growth and learning." Our latest book for our office book club was Start With Why, by Simon Sinek. In a recent lunch and learn, the team was discussing the book when I walked in. I overheard the discussion. They were comparing Apple and Hewlett-Packard.

They discussed the fact that both companies sell computers, but there is something special about how Apple packages their products. "Apple makes it an experience," Trecia said. "That is the same with our practice. Patients can go to any dental office, but they choose us because of the experience. We are the Apple of dentistry!"

Normally, I would have been there and taking part in the discussion, but I happened to be out that day for parent-teacher conferences. And upon returning, I heard this lively discussion. It was exciting to me because it was a real example of our core values and culture in action. The team didn't need me around to adhere to our core values. The core values are a part of them.

We knew that by creating these values and living them out every day, we would be successful in achieving our vision to be the leading dental practice known for Delivering WOW. The next key would be in putting in systems for consistency.

You see, once you put in core values, and your team understands the why behind them, magic starts to happen. Everyone knows the rules of the game, and your team knows what sort of culture they are part of — a culture of success!

DELIVERING WOW ACTION ACTIVITY

Evaluate your core values. Are these core values practiced every day in your office? If not, it's time to get your team together and plan! Don't have written core values in place? Brainstorm with your team to create a new set of core values and discuss why each core value is significant.

CHAPTER 7

Team

While all of the six elements of the Delivering WOW experience are essential, the team holds a special place of significance. Hiring is perhaps one of the biggest decisions you will have to make! The types of hires you make will affect your overall business, including how your company delivers the core values and the culture you develop.

Before we discuss the team, let's consider your role as the leader of your team.

Being a strong leader is critical, as the leader will provide the direction for the team and will set the tone. Your job as a leader is not to know all of the answers, but to attract the right people to get the job done. Your responsibility is to inspire your team, to put in tools for their training, and to ensure they know precisely what you want.

Leading your team

No matter if you own your practice, or are currently working as an associate, the key to having a super productive team who follows systems and delivers Wow is to be a strong leader. Strong leaders are very clear about what is required of the team and are not afraid to let them know. Strong leaders demand excellence and inspire their team by what they have done for the individual team members, patients, and the community. Strong leaders build other leaders.

When you choose to become a Delivering WOW

practice, then it's important that you begin on a path of personal development. Work on growing personally, and not just professionally. Turn your car into a driving university. Listen to podcasts, books on Audible, or other educational material as you commute. Join a mastermind with other dentists who are taking action. Hire a coach. I have worked with a coach and am now part of a mastermind to stretch my thinking to the next level, contribute my areas of expertise, and learn from others. Masterminds are also an excellent way to find people who can hold you accountable.

Here are 7 key areas to master if you want to become an exceptional leader of your practice:

1. Communication. As a leader with a vision, it's imperative that you share your vision, your ideas, and your core values with your team. If you find that you are having a hard time getting people to fall in line with the practice's vision or with an idea you have, then it's very likely that you are not communicating as effectively as you can. Inspire your team to see just how phenomenal the practice can be when the patients are Wowed, and the business is profitable. Make sure that your team understands the benefits of aligning with the company's vision. You'll have a hard time transforming into a Wow practice if you can't communicate this desire and vision.

2. Commitment. It's important to commit to your goals, take action, and then follow through. To achieve your vision, you might have to make some significant changes in how you do business. Because the transition may not be easy, you'll need to be prepared to commit

to this new path. It may require adjustments that some on your team, at first, may not embrace. You may even lose some team members who don't share your vision. If you are wishy-washy and can't commit, then your team will see this, and there will be confusion and a lack of interest in following through on the changes. You must lead by example, so your team sees you are in this for the long haul. The Delivering WOW experience starts with you, as the leader. You must be willing to stick by the decision you've made, no matter what.

3. Confidence. Not every day at the practice will be great. That's true of your business, and it's true in life. But if something goes wrong, do not panic. Be the leader of your team and create an action plan to get things back on track. Create a system. A Delivering WOW team will support you when you need it and work extra hard to help the business grow.

4. Honesty. Honesty is an essential component of leadership. Once you are honest with your team, they will relate more to you and trust you. For example, many times dentists are struggling to control expenses, but the team does not know. Be honest with your team and they will do their part to help control costs. Honesty is what inspires trust. If your team is to trust you, then honesty must be evident. This isn't just about what you say; it's what you do. What you say and do must match up. Being honest will help you build your team because the team will feel it can trust you to do what you say. Simple ways you can show honesty: Uphold your promises. If you say you will do something, do it. If you make a mistake or find you can't keep your promise, own up to it.

5. Decisiveness. Decisiveness means being able to evaluate a situation and make a decision. While this sounds simple, many people have a hard time here. They don't want to make a choice, and so they keep putting off making a decision or keep going back on the decision that was made. What this does is creates chaos and confusion in the practice. It also makes it difficult for your practice to move forward, as there is no real commitment to decisions. If you want to be a good leader, make a point of being decisive. Weigh the options before you make a decision. Don't drag the decision out seemingly forever. This doesn't mean you must make rash choices, or make snap decisions without proper consideration. But it does mean that you should consider the situation, make a decision, and then act accordingly.

6. Intelligence. If you want to be a good leader, then you'll need to show your team that you have the mental power to make sound choices. This doesn't mean you must be a genius or you must be the smartest person in the room. But it does say that you know how to get the information you need to make decisions and that you have the smarts to put the right people in place to makes choices in what you delegate. And that brings us to ...

7. Delegation. As a leader, you must be able to delegate. Many small business owners, and dentists in particular, are stressed out because they just do not delegate. They feel as if they must do all the work themselves. But that's no way to grow. You can't scale your operation if you refuse to delegate. I understand that one of the reasons some of us don't delegate is that

we feel as if no one can do the work as we can. And that may be true. But it's possible to delegate to someone who can do the job in his or her way, and also produce an excellent result. You might even find that the person does the task better than you ever could. Delegation is important if you are to be an effective leader because delegation can help you focus on those essential tasks that only you can do. Once you start to delegate, you will also have more freedom and less stress because not everyone is counting on you to make all of the decisions.

Creating a WOW team

When you commit to building a Wow team, you will need to look for people who are a good fit for your practice's culture. Not every applicant will fit into the culture. Individuals who are just looking for a paycheck or who are not willing to do whatever it takes to get the job done won't be a good fit. Nor complainers. Even one team member with a poor attitude or poor work ethic can put a strain on your practice.

When you commit to becoming a Delivering WOW practice, you're not just looking for ordinary employees. You are looking for star team members. Every team member must be a star and add value. It is vital for you and your team to realize that every position is critical to having the practice achieve its vision. Team members must know that if you did not need certain tasks to be done, then you would have no reason to pay a wage for the tasks to be completed.

Perhaps you already have employees and you wonder how they will fit into the Delivering WOW practice you are now transforming your business into. The best way to help people who are already a part of your practice make the transition is to involve them in the process. Explain the vision and the transformation you are expecting to see in the workplace, and how it will benefit them. Be sure to show that you welcome them on the journey. And then create the conditions to help them grow along with you, so they become Wow team members.

As you are redefining your vision, some of your current team members may feel that this transformation may be too much work, and that's OK. Not every person may want to be a part of your vision. I had one lady who said that this would be too much work. I understood and informed her that this is the new path for the practice, and I was OK if she didn't want to be a part of it. She found another practice that was a better fit. Notice, I was a strong leader and did not let a team member's resistance influence my decision to redefine my practice. I pressed ahead with all of the extremely motivated team members who were ready to Wow.

Here are some key ways you can help your employees become a Wow team:

1. Communicate your vision. Be sure to explain your vision and show how they fit into it. It's important that your team feels included and sees their role. Let them know they are significant in this transformation.

Invest in your team's development. Just as you are growing personally and professionally, so should your team. Facilitate this growth by providing tools and resources. Consider providing Kindles to your team to fast-track their learning. I did this at my office, and it has been amazing to see team members reading the recommended books and excitedly discussing what they learned.

Three great team reads are The Compound Effect by Darren Hardy, Eat That Frog! by Brian Tracy, and What Got You Here Won't Get You There by Marshall Goldsmith. If you would like a FREE audio copy of any of these books, you can download it through my partnership with Audible at http://www.deliveringwow.com/audible.

2. Create team incentives. It's important to incentivize. When you have a Wow team, those team members should feel the benefits that come along with that! Look at ways you can incentivize your team. One way we have incentivized team members in our office is by sharing profits with them. I have provided a share of the profits to team members as bonuses, over and above their regular pay. This is a way that we can all share in the growth of the company. When the team delivers Wow, they get some right back! If you do decide to provide a bonus to your team, make sure that it is based on profits and not production or collections.

3. Recognize team members. While it can be good to offer monetary incentives the whole team can receive and share in, most times this is not necessary. If you are a great leader and your team shares in your vision, they will perform. I constantly "brag" about my team in front of patients. We also share quite a bit about our team's accomplishments on our social media pages. Some fun things that we have done to reward the team are spa days and painting parties. Once we surprised our team with a shopping spree where we later met for lunch, and they shared what they bought for themselves.

4. If you are creating a Wow team, then it's important for team members to know what you expect of them. Be sure to define each person's role and responsibilities. Don't assume they know. Unclear roles and responsibilities are at the heart of many inefficient and ineffective workplaces. Don't let this be the case for yours. When you clearly define and communicate these roles and responsibilities, team members have a better chance of living up to — and exceeding — your expectations.

Many small business owners, including dentists, believe the salary or wage they provide is a reward or incentive enough for their employees. But this is simply not true. And if this is your approach, then it is shortsighted, and it will cost you. Taking care of your employees is an important part of your job when you are a Delivering WOW practice because it is your employees — your team members — who will take care of your customers. If you aren't treating your employees well, don't expect them to treat your customers well.

When you take care of your employees and make them feel connected to the vision, they will give you 200 percent because they know they are part of the process of growing the business. They get excited and happy when they are Delivering WOW. They get invested in creating big wins for the practice. When patients come back, your employees get excited. When certain goals are met, your employees feel proud.

A new approach to hiring

One of the top ways that we have been able to grow a

phenomenal team is by looking at each role in the office, and then deciding which personality style might be the best fit for that position. For example, we have two ladies who work at the front desk. One is responsible for being the big personality who welcomes every patient when they arrive. She knows details about patients' families and loves to chat to make them feel at home. She is the one who has fun with the patients and has no fear asking for video testimonials. The other lady is very detail- oriented.

She answers all patient emails and appointment requests very eloquently and quickly and is responsible for going over treatment plans in a systematic way and auditing patient ledgers.

They have two entirely different personality styles, but both are critical to the success of the front office. When filling these positions, we knew which personality style would be the best fit for each, so we personality profiled our candidates to get the best fit. This meant that when filling the position for the extroverted front desk position, we could not hire a quiet, shy person, so there was no need to interview that personality style. A shy person would not be a good fit. We also took this approach when hiring an assistant for my high-energy, enthusiastic hygienist. Her assistant had to possess the calm, compassionate personality style to support our fearful patients.

One resource I have found helpful is The DISC profile, devised by psychologist Dr. William Moulton Marston. It includes four components and is a tool to measure behavioral styles. It is a personal assessment tool used by individuals to analyze their behavioral patterns and how they could influence their overall personality at work and at different levels in the career ladder. It also helps one understand the behavioral patterns of those whom we deal with in the business world or in day-to-day life.

DISC profile includes the following components:

1. Dominance (D)

Confidence is the key trait in such a person falling in this category. A strong emphasis on achievement of results and goal orientation are the common practices of these individuals. They can be straightforward and blunt, open toward diversity, and adventurous by nature, accepting any challenging situation coming their way.

2. Influence (I)

These individuals are said to be great leaders. They influence others and take charge of situations, but they take along everyone with them. Relationship-oriented and persuasive by nature, these people are very collaborative and see the brighter picture in any situation.

3. Steadiness (S)

Individuals falling into this category are persistent in their behavior. They don't like to be rushed or pushed beyond limits as they exhibit a calm demeanor. They emphasize cooperation, and to a certain extent, they do adjust to unusual circumstances, dealing with things in a subtle manner. They are very supportive of their colleagues and subordinates and are humble and down to earth.

4. Conscientiousness (C)

The name says it all; these individuals are focused on accuracy and quality of work produced along with emphasis on their competencies. They enjoy being trusted and given responsibility as it means for them independence. They are detail-oriented individuals with sound reasoning and expertise. They are perfectionists who dread being wrong.

All of our applicants, as part of their interview process, receive a pre-interview questionnaire and a quick personality profile test so we have a better feel before we offer them an in-office interview. Visit www.deliveringwow.com/newhire to get a copy of the questionnaire and personality profile assessment form.

Your Delivering WOW team will help drive practice goals

To grow every year, I create a budget. I do this to track revenue and expenses as well as to track profitability. Last year I set a revenue goal for the year and then broke that down into monthly goals. I then looked at all of the services that we provide — cleanings, fillings, crowns, whitening, root canals, etc. I reviewed how many procedures were done in each category on average for the prior year and created targets per category, which would allow me to reach my revenue goal. We began putting in goals — the number of each service that we wanted to provide monthly and tracked them daily on whiteboards. The team told me, “Doc, those numbers look a little high. They’re not realistic.” But I pushed on.

I said, "No, guys, we can do it."

That first month, we met all of the targets except for one. The second month we met all of our goals. By the third month, we knew we could go even higher. In fact, I saw my office manager erasing the goals and putting in new targets that were 25 percent higher! Inviting my team to be a part of transforming the practice was amazing because it incentivized them to try harder at all they did.

That is the power of making your team feel like an important part of what you are doing. They work to meet and exceed goals, sometimes even setting higher goals themselves.

But it's not just about meeting and exceeding goals. Building the right team is also about the feelings of respect and connection that grow. One day I walked into the office, and one of my dental assistants said she had a dream about me.

She gave me a hug and said, "I just want to tell you, this is the best job ever. Thank you so much for the opportunity to be part of this team."

In another example, a dental assistant who saw a Facebook post that we were looking for a dental assistant because our team was growing called every day saying, "I have to be a part of this incredible team!" She was hired and is super committed to our core values and our vision.

This new hire has been phenomenal.

I'll sometimes put my head around the corner and see a team member giving an arm and hand massage to a patient. The team member will look up and our eyes might connect. We just smile. There is a particular bond in this work of Wow. That is the environment we have, and that is the team we have.

Going to work is fun for us. Patients can sense it. They feel it. They tell me this all the time. That's why I can't stop talking about my team. I walked in one day recently, and they had come up with a team vision statement. It was about supporting each other. I love it!

You may have noticed that I refer to my staff as my team. That is because we are a team, working together for a common goal — which is the fulfillment and maintenance of the vision. We have a sense of camaraderie and respect for one another. Consider how you think of your team members, and commit to working together to achieve the vision.

DELIVERING WOW ACTION ACTIVITY

Have a close look at your current team, and make sure they are aligned with your vision. If not, have a discussion with them about the importance of all team members being committed to the vision. If they are not willing to commit, let them know that it is OK to choose another office that might be a better fit.

•

Subscribe to the Delivering WOW Dental Podcast in iTunes as well as other podcasts to scale up your learning. Download the Audible app to start turning your car into a driving university. Join the Delivering WOW Dental Hangout, our free Facebook Group at www.deliveringwowhangout.com to mastermind with other top dentists around the world who are taking action to get results.

CHAPTER 8

Systems

Would you be willing to make one single, simple change in your practice, if it would guarantee that you could regularly meet 80-90 percent of your daily revenue goal by lunchtime?

Most likely, you are saying yes to this question. Of course, you would be willing to make one single, simple change if it could have such a dramatic impact on how much you earn.

Well, that's what this chapter is all about. It's about changing the way you do business, so you get to a more efficient and profitable way of running your practice. The single change: Systems.

Many companies lack the proper systems to produce the massive results they want. However, by systematizing your practice, you can boost results and create actionable steps to reach your goals.

Systems also ensure consistency and accuracy and allow all of your team members to know exactly what they must do.

Once you have systems, the systems can run the practice, and you can create more time for what matters most or for what you have defined in your personal vision.

Let me give you one example of a single, simple change we made. We created a system for block scheduling. That was the change I mentioned at the start of this chapter.

Here is the specific block-scheduling plan we used. If you follow these steps, you too will be amazed at the results:

1. Create three morning blocks on your schedule. In my case they are from 8:00 a.m. to 9:00 a.m., 9:00 am to 10:00 a.m., and 10:00 a.m. to 12:00 p.m.

2. Blocks can only be filled with four or more fillings, a crown, veneers, implants, or a combination of the above. I do not do root canals, but they could be placed in a block as well.

3. For those patients requiring a longer block, they can take the two-hour block from 10:00 a.m. to 12:00 p.m., or they can take two one-hour blocks (8:00 a.m. to 9:00 a.m. and 9:00 a.m. to 10:00 a.m.).

4. Cements, follow-ups, consults, and single fillings are not to be placed in these blocks.

5. One morning of the week and every afternoon are not blocked to accommodate one to three fillings, cements, adjustments, consults, etc.

6. If appointment blocks are free for the next day, they can be released after 1 p.m. If lab cases come in that day, we will call to schedule those patients in these released spots. Patients love if they can get back in quickly to cement their cases.

Once we started offering every patient who had four or more fillings and/or a combination of crowns to do all work in one day, we were amazed at the results. What we heard was "Of course I'd prefer one visit. Why would I want to come back several times?" That was very interesting. We also now offer to do treatment on both sides in one visit. Yes it means that patients might be numb on both sides, but we just inform them that it should be back to normal in 2-3 hours, so they know what to expect. Oral surgeons numb both sides all the time and advise patients what to expect, and we do the same. Our hygienists also offer to do full mouth scaling and root planing in one visit, and the patients love it. They don't have to come back to go through the process again.

This system has been a game-changer for my practice because it allows us to schedule longer, more detailed procedures in the morning. It provides added convenience to patients because they no longer have to figure out how to fit in multiple dental visits. It lets me schedule longer procedures in the early part of the day, when my eyes are fresh.

Additionally, block scheduling decreases overhead costs, as there are less setups throughout the day. We can reduce the cost of sterilization bags, needles, water, disinfectant, and electricity. This new way of scheduling also lets me work fewer clinical hours. What used to take two and a half hours seeing five patients 30 minutes apart for one filling can now be done in one hour. And, it makes it possible to earn 80-90 percent of the day's revenue by lunchtime.

Yes, that's one simple change in how we schedule appointments. Creating a block scheduling system has allowed us to increase our efficiency, revenue, and client satisfaction.

That's the power of a well-placed system.

Why do we need systems?

Systems are essential to delivering a Wow experience. Systems help to create consistency so patients can count on the same results and the same experience on every visit. But systems aren't just for creating a consistent experience for patients. Systems help to create workplace efficiency, so you can get more done with less.

Systems may be an intimidating idea for some business owners and dentists, but actually understanding the benefits of systems can transform your practice. When I began implementing systems, I started to experience significant growth. You just cannot grow the way you want if you refuse to implement systems in your practice.

Not every system has to be complicated, and indeed, many of those in our office are not. Systems are simple, standardized ways of doing things. If there is a problem or breakdown in our office, I can often determine the breakdown happened because there was no clarity with the system surrounding it or there was no system in place.

Some of the first areas where I standardized and implemented systems were to create manuals for all positions, minimum quantity lists to manage inventory and supplies, and written scripts for how we would answer the telephone, patient emails, and Facebook questions.

Let's explore systems and why you need them in

your practice.

So which systems?

Anytime you have an activity that is repeatable, meaning you will do it over and over again, then it should have a system. Some common places where you need systems in your practice are in generation of new patients, tracking referrals and marketing campaigns, collection of patient feedback, management of supplies, patient follow-up, and the patient experience.

All of these are repeatable activities that lend themselves to systemization.

It becomes inefficient and ineffective to continue to perform these operations in an ad hoc way where there is no consistency. This also lends itself to inconsistent results, as the lack of standardization of the process can sometimes mean a particular activity is performed in one way, and the next time it is completed in a different way.

So how do you implement systems?

Creating systems and processes to manage the flow of tasks at your office will increase your productivity and reduce costs. You will find there are many automated systems you can implement that reduce or eliminate the need for deep human involvement. Some systems, such as patient appointment reminders, can be automated through the use of an email auto responder that is set to send out a reminder email to the patient for a subsequent appointment based on a set trigger, such as a set period. Other systems may actions, such as a system to colle Your patient feedback system m end of an appointment, whereby y an easy way of providing feedbacl

Here are some tips for implementing systems in your practice:

1. Create an operations manual with pictures. Write down all of the operations you perform in your office within this handbook. Your operations manual will help ensure that your office is not dependent on any one person. This is important because if a team member leaves, then all the institutional knowledge of how to perform a particular set of tasks does not leave with that person. A new hire can simply pick up a copy of the manual and know exactly what is expected of them and how to perform the required tasks for their position. Once things are written down, your office is no longer dependent on your constant presence on a daily basis. You can delegate responsibilities and be assured tasks will be completed according to your standardized manual. Having systems documented in an operations manual also has the benefit of allowing you to have a standardized way of judging employee performance.

The operations manual is an impartial gauge of how each member is doing. If someone is not performing according to the manual, then you can see that. Also, if someone is following the manual but is not getting the results you expect, then it is easy to walk through the process with the person to see where exactly he or she ssing a step.

2. Create a KPI chart. Write down what each team member must do daily, weekly, and monthly and create a chart that can be posted in your office. This key performance indicators chart helps to define responsibilities, as well as create a standardized way of keeping track of those responsibilities. KPIs, including charts, contribute to measuring your business's performance in critical areas. Your chart that includes team member responsibilities can help to see how employees are performing, as well as show what needs to be done, in the event an employee is out sick, on vacation, or leaves your practice.

3. Use checklists for all tasks. Checklists ensure there is consistency and there is clarity for all tasks that must be completed for each position. This means you are providing further standardization of your processes when each team member follows the same checklist for repeatable tasks. It might seem like a lot of work to use checklists, but checklists allow you to focus on what matters most.

4. Complete a policies and procedures manual. A policies and procedures manual helps to address and answer common and uncommon workplace questions, such as employee leave, opening and closing the office for the day, etc. Often policies and procedures are not implemented or developed until they have become issues. Creating this manual is aimed at helping you put your policies and procedures in place before you

need them.

The main point you want to remember about systems is that you want to standardize as much as you can when it comes to the repeatable activities you engage in regularly. This standardization takes the guesswork and variability out of your results.

We have even created a system for referrals. Each patient who sends a referral as well as the person being referred gets $10 off a future visit. Once someone refers five or more patients, they become a member of our VIP rewards program, and they receive 5 percent off all future visits. This referral program is part of a word-of-mouth inspired marketing system. When we Wow patients, they go out and evangelize for us. They are out there talking about us, which is, in turn, bringing us more business. Every Wow we offer is a system for growing. None of the Wows is an isolated instance. Each is wrapped in a system so that we can consistently deliver that Wow.

When you commit to becoming a Delivering WOW practice, systems can also help you get to the massive growth you seek. Systems help answer the question of, "How do I reach my target?"

For instance, as I mentioned in an earlier chapter, we track services on a whiteboard. We make a list of all of the services that we offer and the target number that we would like to achieve for that month. Every day we update the total number of each service month-to-date with a red dry erase marker and compare it with our goal. Once we meet our goal, we change the actual number from red to green. This system also has us to evaluate our target mid-month, and if it looks like we may not reach our goal, we can change the dynamics of the month by offering a Facebook promotion or writing an educational piece in a patient newsletter for that particular service.

If you set a target of a revenue goal for the year, you can systematize how you're going to get there. Putting a system to every service you offer is how you can get there. Having goals doesn't mean that you are diagnosing anything new. It means that you are asking better questions to find out what your patients want so that you can provide the solutions to their problems. It means that your phone scripts are so vibrant that prospective new patients know that you are the right dentist to provide their solutions. It means that you do whatever it takes to start same-day treatment if the patient is ready versus putting them off to another day. This whiteboard system holds you accountable for being consistent in your case presentations so that patients will schedule their needed treatment. This one system alone increased our revenue by $20,000 in one month!

A system for getting to your patient's *why*

When your patient comes to your practice, it is important that you understand why they are there. What are they looking for? What is their why? Are they looking for crowns or do they want peace of mind that their tooth won't break while on vacation? Are they looking for scaling and root planing, or do they wish to ensure that their teeth won't get long or loose? Do they want veneers or teeth whitening, or is it that they want self-confidence? Once you know your patient's why, you can ask better questions to provide solutions to their problems.

The best way to find your patient's why is to ask open-ended questions. Questions like, "What is your immediate concern?" "Why is that of concern?" "Which side do you want to start first?" "Would you like to schedule this week or next week?" Notice, none of these questions could be answered with yes or no. Each question would require the patient to give details of what they want and why.

One of the most frequent questions that I like to ask is, "What is your resistance?" I ask this when patients say they don't want braces, or they don't want to do a root canal. When you ask this simple question, people tell you their real story. Perhaps their spouse lost a tooth because they had a root canal and did not do the crown. If they share that story, you can explain the real reason they lost the tooth. Perhaps they don't want braces because of the look of the metal, not knowing that ceramic brackets are an option. Perhaps, their child is getting married next month, and their resources are tied up with funding the event. Perhaps they are moving in two months, and they don't that realize you can complete their crowns in plenty of time before they leave. Once you know your patients' resistances, you can speak to those and answer their questions. Once people have clarity, they can make a decision to move forward and accept your recommended treatment.

Listen to understand what patients want — and then deliver it

A good way to find out what your patients want is to ask them. Yes, that's it. Ask and listen. This is a pretty simple approach, but it's also pretty uncommon. Often, as dentists, we believe we know what our patients want, or we try to tell them what they want. So we deliver what we think they would like, rather than focus on delivering what they want.

And how often do we actually listen to understand? Often, we are listening to respond. The difference is stark. Listening to respond is what we naturally do. We listen, waiting so we can jump in and share our opinions and ideas. Often, we are not even really listening to what the other person is saying, as we are so focused on our own thoughts and formulating our replies. All we care about is the response we will make. As the leader of your dental practice, it's important that you listen, ask a question for clarification, and then respond to their reply.

Have you ever had a patient tell you that they wanted to fix their front tooth, but you can't stop focusing on that bombed out #19? Well, this happens all the time. It's like going to a clothing store and you want to buy a purple suit, and the salesclerk keeps offering you a blue one. Perhaps because she thinks that blue is more practical.

But what she fails to realize is that your favorite color is purple, you are going to a wedding, and you want to make a statement. What she should have done was sell you the purple suit and ask you if you want to get a blue one as well.

The same concept applies to dentistry. Listen to your patient and you will fix their front tooth, the bombed out molar, and get all of their family and friends as well! Otherwise, your patient who was fixing their front tooth to go to their best friend's wedding just might go somewhere else.

When you conduct surveys to learn how you can better serve your patients, listen. Better yet, write down their recommendations and decide if these are things you can easily implement. Placing toothbrushes in the bathroom was one suggestion by a patient. Another patient told us that although she likes all of the fancy gourmet teas, she wanted good old-fashioned Jamaican tea, like Ginger and Cerasee. How easy do you think it was to integrate these requests? Super. And the results? Well, it gave our patients something to talk about and showed that we were listening.

Systems can make sure you're not overlooking something essential

Here is a real example of why you need systems, even for things that seem obvious. One challenge of living here in Jamaica is that there are often droughts. So there are water restrictions. Many times the water supply is completely shut off. As a result of it, people have water tanks that hold water for their homes or businesses. One day I was working and the dental chair completely shut off. I thought, "Okay, that's just very strange."

What I found out shortly after that is that our water tanks had completely emptied! As a result of this, the compressor and suction did not work. We had to close the business the rest of the day. We had to have water delivered by a private company to fill up the tank. I have someone who tidies up the office. I assumed that he was watching the water levels in the tank. However, as you can see, no one was checking.

I didn't get upset. I said, "Guys, you know what that means?"

And they said, "We need a system."

So we made a system. Every day during a drought, at 12 o'clock, Mr. David looks into our tank to make sure there is enough water to supply us for the next day.

What may have happened in the past was that I might have gotten very upset or frustrated because we ran out of water. But I didn't react that way. I knew that it happened because there was no system.

Assigning ownership of a system

Decide who will be responsible for the implementation of systems. Most times this should not be the business owner. What the team needs, however, are clearly defined KPIs, the proper training, and deadlines. They also need someone to hold them accountable. In my practice, the person who holds the team accountable is the office manager. The office manager helps to ensure that broken elements of a system get recognized, documented, and addressed.

Set aside time to review your business goals and performance, and to evaluate whether the systems you've put in place have the impact you desire. Review this with the person you've assigned to own your systems. In my practice, I have a weekly 30-minute meeting every Monday morning to discuss systems and projects that my office manager is currently overseeing.

I attribute our overall success to the Delivering WOW experience, but I must give special credit to systems.

Systems are critical to achieving big result
increase your revenue by $20,000 in a mon
tracking a system you can put the focus on th
I know that it has worked for us.

Testing and measuring systems and processes

Keeping track of your KPIs, systems, and other critical methods of measuring or facilitating growth is essential. If you neglect to keep track of your key performance indicators, systems, and other important methods of measuring and facilitating growth, then you won't know when you are progressing or experiencing a setback. If something is not working, don't blame your people, create a system. Your training manual should be so detailed that anyone can walk into your business and be able to have a smooth, consistent transition.

It is critical to know your numbers and understand your profits and losses, which should be documented within your financial system. Your financial system should document your revenue, expenses, and profits. Many teach that profit is what you get to keep after all of your expenses are paid. However, I like to think of it a different way. I like to think of profit first and take my profit first. I pull out a percentage of revenue each week and shift it into a profit account and run my business on the rest. An excellent book on this topic is Profit First by Mike Michalowicz. (Mike and I discussed this concept on the Delivering WOW Dental Podcast Episode 18.)

To run a lean business, you also have to think about strategies to increase revenue, such as increasing new patient numbers and having more patients to complete recommended treatment. You also have to look at your expenses.

One of the easiest ways to cut expenses is to look at your supply costs. We used a Google search to cost compare all of the materials that we use in our office with an online supplier. We discovered that we were able to cut supplies by 30 percent. We sent this list to our top supplier, who offered to beat the online supplier's price. We then shifted our printing services and our graphics work to online suppliers. We also decided to look at different labs that would provide excellent quality at a lower cost. One area that we did not cut, however, was our budget for our team.

Are there expenses you are incurring because you don't have a system in place to handle that operation? Cutting costs by using your financial system to evaluate where you are can help you have more profits to grow. Another great tip when purchasing equipment is to ask, "Is this the best price?" Most times it is not, and the salesperson or supplier will reduce the cost to accommodate the sale.

Some Tips for Testing and Measuring Within Your Practice:

1. Complete and work from monthly budgets. Budgets help you plan expenses. When you work with a budget, you can plan purchases, repairs, and more. A budget also lets you know where you may be paying too much in your business.

2. Set your fees based on desired profit margins not on what feels right or what others are charging. When creating your fee schedule, determine what your fixed

costs break down to per hour and half hour. This means adding up all utilities, rent, salaries, etc., for the month and dividing that figure by the number of production hours per month. You must also take into account your variable expenses, including dental supplies used and lab costs per procedure. In my practice, we have even broken supply costs down to the amount spent per cotton roll for each procedure. Add the fixed costs per hour or half hour plus the variable costs for each procedure. Then, and only then, should you set your fees. Decide what profit margin you would like to make then set your fees. When was the last time you raised your prices? A price increase may be necessary and instantly improves margin.

3. Keep a record of your profit margins and compare from month to month. This helps you evaluate the growth you are making, as well as the overall health of your dental practice.

4. Track and measure the source for all new patients. Your system for lead generation should allow you to track and measure the leads you have coming into your business. Where are they coming from? What are the best sources for receiving new patients? Are there any sources that used to work but are no longer working?

5. Track your conversion of leads to customers. Getting a steady stream of leads is essential to any business. But converting those leads into new patients who are paying customers is the actual test of how well your offer matches the needs of those you are attracting. So how well are you converting those leads into new patients? Which lead source produces a better

conversion rate?

6. Measure key performance indicators for all areas of the company. While there may be many key performance indicators you keep track of, based on goals for each position, there should be a few essential ones you monitor to be sure you are progressing toward your overall goals.

Here are some key financial metric percentages for dental practices:

- Staff salaries (25%-30% of overall budget)
- Lab fees (6%-8% of overall budget)
- Facility (5%-7% of overall budget)
- Dental supplies (5%-8% of overall budget)
- Marketing (5%-7% of overall budget)
- Operating expenses (10%-12% of overall budget)

You can also track the following:

- Number of new patients
- Number of calls received for each procedure vs. the percentage scheduled
- Number of new patients per referral source — including percentage from existing patients and social media
- Number of procedures completed per service category
- Percentage of treatment plans converted

7. Measure your average dollar sale per patient. Knowing how much you earn per patient is a key metric that can help you grow. Once you know the average dollar sale per patient, you can look for small ways to increase it. These small increases can spell big growth for your business over time. Great ways to increase your

average dollar sale are by providing same-day services such as adult and child sealants and fluoride as well as selling products that can add value, such as electronic toothbrushes, fluoride, and water flossers. You should also ask each patient if they want to start today. We are not always able to work in same-day treatment. However, after testing and measuring we decided to add additional assistants to be able to work in more same-day treatment. These assistants accommodate the setup, patient education, and making of temporaries while I am finishing treatment in the next room.

8. Test and measure every marketing campaign. Testing and measuring your marketing campaigns helps you determine your return on investment. This can help you decide which marketing activities are most effective for you. You may find that a commonly accepted marketing activity isn't giving you the results you think they are, once you start testing and measuring. Eliminate what is not working, and scale up what is.

9. Do an analysis of your supply costs quarterly. Analyzing your supply costs on a quarterly basis helps to ensure you are getting the best price. Don't assume that a supplier that was once the best option for you, still is. The costs of supplies can change often, so analyzing what you are spending can help you take advantage of price drops.

10. Negotiate with your suppliers. We often assume the stated price is the only price there is. Most times, this is simply not the case. Negotiate with your suppliers to get lower rates or better terms. If you regularly purchase a high volume, for instance, then you may be able to

negotiate a volume discount. Or if you have a history of paying on time, then that may have negotiation leverage that can help you get a better rate or better terms in some way.

11. Know your fixed expenses per hour. Knowing your fixed expenses per hour is important because it can help you determine if you are offering the right services and rates, as well as where you need to make improvements. Knowing fixed expenses can also let you know when it's time to hire, as payroll is often the biggest expense for many dental practices.

12. Know your breakeven point. The breakeven point lets you know when you start to make a profit (or when you are operating at a loss). Your breakeven point is simply the point at which the cost of running your business is equal to the revenue you are bringing into the business. When you are bringing in more revenue than it costs you, then you have exceeded the breakeven point and turned a profit. When you are bringing in less revenue than it costs you, then you are operating at a loss. Knowing your breakeven point will influence buying and operating decisions.

When you are looking for massive growth, testing and measuring in these areas is critical. This will provide the information you need to help make decisions about purchases, operations, and more. All of these tested elements should be part of a system.

When you begin standardizing processes and implementing systems, you will be surprised at just how much duplication of effort you can eliminate, how efficient you can become, and how much more time you will have to dedicate to other tasks.

DELIVERING WOW ACTION ACTIVITY

Go back over this chapter and consider what you can do now to begin implementing systems. Look at your business. Make a list of all of the systems you want to implement this year and break them down into what you will do each quarter, then each month.

CHAPTER 9

Brand

You have finally decided to book your dream vacation. You're going to Italy! You're excited about the trip and can't wait to get there. With your flight already set, you're ready to book your hotel. You look up a few travel sites to see what's available. The first hotel that catches your eye is a great deal! It actually falls a little below your budget. You start thinking about all of the extra shopping and sightseeing you can do with the extra money. Your mind even begins to drift to the wine tour you would like to take. Then you look at the reviews. The reviews are all 2-3 stars. The pictures of the hotel are OK, but nothing special. Then you move on to the next hotel on the page. This hotel is slightly over your budget, but is beautiful and even includes free breakfast and Wi-Fi. You notice that every review is a 5 star, and all of the testimonials boast about the incredible location, fantastic service, and the phenomenal experience you receive as a guest.

It costs more than the other, but which do you book?

There is a good chance you would book the more expensive hotel. Why? Because its brand is better. Its photos are welcoming and attractive. The reviews are fantastic. The amenities are exceptional.

That is the power of a brand.

So what is a brand? A brand is what people say about you when you are not around. As it relates to your business, your brand is all about the stories that people tell their friends and family when they describe your practice. It's not about a business card. It's not about a logo. It's about the emotional connection that people have with your business. Once your practice has a fascinating culture and consistent systems, then the result is that when people talk about your practice, they say "Wow!" "Wow, they see me on time." "Wow, that was the best experience ever." "Wow, I didn't feel the injection." "Wow, they give back to charity." "Wow, Wow, Wow!"

Having a great brand means that people can't stop talking about your business. It means that you have "Raving Fans." Having a remarkable brand where people can't stop talking about you means you have climbed to the top of the ladder. No company that has a phenomenal brand got there by accident. They all started by creating a vision and by focusing not on the competition, but on being unique. They all described their company story through their culture, developed core values, invested in their team, and made sure that systems were put in place.

Many small business owners believe the price is the determining factor in customers' decisions, and that's most often not the case. While the price may be a factor, it's often not the deciding factor. As I showed in the example that started this chapter, we often are looking for certain signals and cues about a business, to determine if we will spend money there. Those signals and cues are conveyed in the brand. If the brand fascinates, we will spend money, even if we could get a lower price somewhere else.

Competing on price is never a winning proposition when you are in business. That is because you can always find someone who is willing to do a task for less. So if you keep driving your price down to compete, you could very well find that it costs you more to deliver the service than you earn from selling it!

A better way to stand out is by creating a fascinating brand. When you create an exciting brand, you are promising and delivering a Wow experience. That means that just going through the motions and being just like every other practice won't do for you. You want more. You want to thrive; you want to fascinate! Delivering WOW may take a bit more work in the beginning as you change your thinking and transform your practice, but it will pay off with higher returns. Once your brand is known for Delivering WOW, your practice will be on autopilot and it can run without you. You will have more time, you will earn more money, and you will have more freedom!

Your dental practice already has a brand; every business does. But that brand may be ordinary and unexceptional before you make the Delivering WOW transformation. If you find that your brand is weak or nondescript right now, don't be discouraged. Many of us have been there. We weren't taught how to build strong brands when we were in dental school. But as we realize we want our practices to be better than they have been, we realize we must do something different!

When you have a Wow brand, then you will find that you attract more customers, and you don't have to compete solely on price. You get to compete on your

Delivering WOW point of distinction.

So what does it mean to have a Wow brand and how do the other elements of the Delivering WOW experience contribute to that brand?

Let's find out.

So what is a Delivering WOW brand?

While I am speaking specifically to dentists in this book, a Delivering WOW brand is something any service business can aspire to have, regardless of industry or niche. A Delivering WOW brand is a brand that promises to fascinate its customers through a phenomenal experience.

So in the context of your practice, what would Delivering WOW mean? I've already shared with you what it means in my practice: It is about intentionally being different and in creating stories for our patients to share. It's about the details of the office tour, music and headphones to take away the sound, hand and arm massages to relax patients before treatment, and unexpected surprises such as hot chocolate for the kids and perfume in the bathroom. It's about calling our patients after treatment and on their birthdays. We even have a "Kids Club" where children are treated to their own newsletter, t-shirts, and water bottles.

These amenities are just some of the features that help contribute to our Wow brand. As you've just read in the chapter on systems, there are also many invisible features that also contribute to our brand. A great example is the process that we take patients through from the first phone call to when we ask them for a video testimonial or a review. (Our tight system ensures that they will say Wow!)

Everything you do in your business contributes to your brand. So if you think it doesn't matter that there is alginate on the floor from your last patient, it does. If you think it doesn't matter that your receptionist doesn't make eye contact and smile, it does. If you think it doesn't matter that you never seem to have tissue in the restroom, it does. Each of these may look like a little thing when the pressure to do so much overwhelms you, but each of these can take away from the brand you are building.

How the other Delivering WOW elements contribute to your brand

As mentioned earlier, your brand is what people say about you when you are not around. Building a fascinating brand does not just happen. It is a result of successfully mastering every step along the way. Here is how the other elements in the Delivering WOW experience contribute to your brand.

Culture is the story that you want to tell the world about your practice. It is made up of how you and your team interact with each other and your patients, the core values you hold, and how you present yourself to the community. Culture influences your brand because if you get it right, you are telling the world what you want your brand to represent.

Core values are the rules of the game of how you develop your brand, and ultimately your vision. Core values influence your brand because they align you with patients who believe in your values. They connect you with your ideal patient.

Team is how your core values will be carried out. They bring the personality to the practice. The team you have interacting with patients will influence your brand because those interactions will determine the quality of the experience customers have with you.

Systems are what allow you to be consistent in delivering your core values. Systems influence your brand because without consistency, none of your new strategies for growing your brand will stick. You may try something new and get super excited, but never follow through.

And of course, your vision clearly defines what the ultimate goal is for the practice, and creating a fascinating brand where you have a practice full of "raving fans" is how you will achieve it.

One night I was relaxing at home with my husband, and a message came to my phone from Melissa, my office manager, that a patient had tagged us in his Twitter post. Once opening the link in the tweet, it was to a blog article that he had written about his experience in our practice. All I could say was Wow! You never realize the importance of every small detail that you put into creating an incredible patient experience until you receive something like this from one of your patients:

Although a bit long, I want to share this blog post by Andre O. Brown (andreobrown.com) in its entirety, as it was at this moment that I knew that we had a magical brand.

Good customer service is always appreciated, and in some lines of business, it may make or break you. A good restaurant can get by with great food, but add good customer service and you'll keep customers coming back. Maybe great service aids digestion. We also like receiving good customer service at stores, at the spa, and at hotels. After all, those are service-oriented establishments aren't they?

Generally speaking, a good customer experience enhances the delivery of many services. However there are some areas where we don't expect good service, and if we do receive it, then it's a noticeable exception. When we're sick, we visit the doctor, but whether or not the doctor has great bedside manner does little to prevent our visit. After all, we aren't going to curl up and die because we don't like how our doctor talks to us. We also expect a long wait and generally accept this as par for the course in the health industry.

We've talked about food and healthcare, both of which we cannot do without. But what about a service that we need, but that we generally don't like and tend to avoid for as long as possible. Ever had a toothache? They don't usually start out chronic do they? However, most of us delay our visits to the dentist until we can't even scream in agony, as the air hitting our teeth would cause further pain.

Visiting the dentist is a uniquely uncomfortable experience. No one likes being prodded and poked in the mouth, with drills and pointed metal instruments. And let's not even get started on the scratching and scraping sounds that give a new meaning to the phrase "setting your teeth on edge." Yet, routinely subjecting ourselves to dental procedures can save us a world of pain. However, that's seldom incentive enough for some of us. Is there anything that could possibly make a dental visit bearable? Believe it or not, one dental practice came up with a brilliant approach.

The Jamaica Cosmetic Dental Services (JCDS) Facebook page tries to lure customers with the promise of a short wait time and "Wow experiences." Generally we expect to wait when we visit the dentist and rightfully use the time to steel ourselves in preparation for the assault against our mouths. However, if you've ever tried to slip a dental visit in on your lunch break, then you know the frustration of long wait periods. So the promise of a 15 minute or less wait is good bait.

Before visiting anywhere, a little research is in order. A quick trip to the JCDS website gives you reason for pause. On the site, you are greeted by the smiling faces of JCDS staff members. The image is reminiscent of sitting back in your dentist's chair, minus the bright white light and gnarly instruments. The image is actually quite pleasant and sets the tone for a visit even before you've decided to go.

Once you've entered the JCDS website, you are greeted by photos not of teeth, tools, or office furniture, but of smiling staff members, children, and community outreach programs. The staff photo in which staff members pose with random things from around the office is worth special mention. One staff member is holding up a sign that says "I love my job," which while unusual is immediately believable because of the sheer fun nature of the photo. These people actually look like they love their jobs!

Another thing stood out on the site: the details of the promise of a "Wow experience." Part of this experience is the promise of a hand massage to relax you before, and music to distract you during, your treatment. By this point, it becomes obvious that these people get something that everyone else has missed: getting people to do something that they don't want to do is possible if you can make the overall experience better. Air travel sucks, but friendly flight attendants can make being stuck in a metal tube for hours slightly more bearable. And no one likes to be reminded that their airplane could fall out of the sky, but fun safety instructions go a long way to making you pay attention. So too, JCDS promises to transform your dental visit with excellent service, and they deliver on this promise!

Getting people to do something that they don't want to do is possible if you can make the overall experience better.

The first think you'll notice when you visit their office is, well, their office. It doesn't feel like a regular dental office. It's spacious and bright. The treatment areas don't have doors, but still maintain privacy while getting rid of annoying door slamming. The usual dental charts are replaced with large beautiful portraits of people. In such a beautiful environment, even the tools look less daunting. And if you're a tea drinker, you will appreciate the gourmet tea in the waiting area. Oh, and there is coffee if you fancy that.

As a new client, instead of being greeted by forms to fill out, your receptionist asks you for basic information and enters it directly into the system. That made registration quick and easy! And you'd better drink your lovely tea quickly, because they do deliver on the promise of the 15 minute or less wait time.

Your first visit starts with a tour of the facility. That's right, a tour. They do everything to distract you from what you're actually there to do. And guess what, it works! After the tour you're taken to the treatment room and talked through your treatment.

One thing that stands out as you interact and speak with the staff is their attentiveness — they seem truly interested in your comfort and well-being, not just in getting the job done. One way that they ensure that you're relaxed and comfortable is by offering you a complimentary hand massage before you start your treatment. But wait, there is more! For many people, the noise of the machines and instruments in their mouth is even more nerve racking than the actual feel of the instruments. Understanding this, and having a desire to make you as comfortable as possible throughout your procedure, the brilliant minds behind JCDS came up with another great distraction. You can listen to music of your choosing, delivered to your ears via headphones throughout your treatment. The relaxing effect of this is not to be underestimated.

After your examination and treatment, you are offered a warm towel. Only after you are comfortably clean does your dentist or an assistant explain what was done and make recommendations for other procedures. Most places stop there. JCDS takes this a step further and prepares a treatment plan that is printed and provided to you before you leave.

On the counter by the reception area is a collection of small signs, including the "I love my job" sign featured in the photo on the website. Nestled in this pile is one sign that epitomizes the experience promised and delivered by JCDS. That sign reads: "We treat people not teeth." That sentence is what truly distinguishes the JCDS experience: they focus not on your cavities, your cleaning, your crown nor your filling. Instead, they focus on you, and everything else falls into place.

It is evident that much thought was put into how to transform a normally unpleasant experience, into one that you no longer dread. From your first contact online to your first visit to the office the overall experience created by JCDS is actually enjoyable and that is quite a feat.

I am very honored that Mr. Brown took the time to share his experience with others. It touches me in a special way to know that all of the work that we are doing is making a difference. His feedback makes my work worthwhile. It shows that what we do really matters.

Create marketing to attract your ideal patients

Marketing is about being remarkable. What makes you different? I see so many dentists place yellow pages and newspaper ads that list all of the services they offer. They say we do cleanings, crowns, extractions, dentures, etc. Well, these are services that most dentists are known for providing. Make sure to be known for more than the services you offer.

Make your ads remarkable! In our print and digital advertising, we discuss our on-time guarantee and that we offer complimentary hand massages. You may think a hand massage would not attract patients. Let me tell you, it does. Another great example of a practice that gets it right is that of orthodontist Dr. Ann Marie Gorczyca. She has a Summer Splash party for her community each year. Everybody knows her practice for that party. People look forward to it the entire year. And guess what? It has nothing to do with Orthodontics.

The way you market plays a role in the brand you build. If your marketing is always about being the low-price option, then you will attract patients who are looking for the lowest price.

If your marketing is about changing lives through beautifying people's smiles, then you will attract lots of people who want to improve their smile. If your marketing is about Delivering WOW experiences, then you will attract people who are fearful or appreciate paying a little extra to be treated like a VIP.

That brings me to Ms. Williams. She is a patient I have had for more than eight years. Ms. Williams has Sjogren's Syndrome and takes three buses to get to our office. Ms. Williams is a retired teacher with no insurance and does not have a lot of money, but she knew that she had a problem because her teeth kept getting cavities. Frustrated, she came to my practice after seeing me on a morning show.

Upon evaluation, she needed a ton of work. Really just about every tooth needed a crown. We segmented her treatment and she saved and did one or two crowns at a time.

Now we are definitely not the least expensive dental practice in town, but she still chose to come. One day I asked her, "Why is it that you choose to come to us? You must pass 10-15 dentists before reaching our office." She simply said, "I just love the way you make me feel!"

Well, I am happy to say that all of Ms. Williams' crowns have been completed. We chose to help her a little along the way, but she was committed because of the patient experience.

Build your marketing around sharing your core values. Focus on your culture and all of the fun that happens behind the scenes. Create the story that will become your brand.

By the way, you don't need a large marketing budget to get results, thanks to the array of marketing options we have available to us today. Marketing costs have gone way down due to the use of the Internet and other creative strategies. In the early part of this book,

I shared some numbers with you: We were able to get 250 new patients in one month with one strategy. In another example, we saw a 1,500 percent return on an ad. Some marketing strategies are winners.

By tracking your return on investment, you will double your efforts on the winners and eliminate the losers.

While there are many ways of marketing your practice, I will discuss some of my favorites here. They are social media, host/beneficiary arrangements, and strategic alliances.

Social media can produce an incredible return on investment

Is your practice on social media? If not, you are missing out on an excellent opportunity to grow your practice. The average American spends 40 minutes per day on Facebook.

This is HUGE!

Facebook has made a significant impact on my practice. We currently receive more than 40 new patients a month from Facebook alone. Facebook is our #1 strategy for external marketing. Why? Because it works. Facebook is where we share our practice story, our culture. People see us having fun and see us impacting so many lives in our community. From Facebook, followers go to our website, they see pictures of our dentists and our team as well as see beautiful before and after photos of our dental work.

We love referrals from Facebook! These new patients walk in already connected — they know us. They feel like we are their personal friends. People buy from people that they like and trust, and acquiring new patients from Facebook builds that confidence.

We currently have an active Facebook page with more than 50,000 Fans, which we have grown one like at a time. We post updates there that show off our culture and spread our brand message. We are known as the fun, friendly office that provides an amazing experience, beautiful dentistry, and gives back to the community.

It's crucial when you are creating your social strategy that you realize that you will not get 1,000 Fans overnight. It starts one Fan at a time. It also starts by creating killer posts that evoke emotion. I have done extensive research on dental practice Facebook pages and have found a few key errors. The first is that many of them lack consistency. They post one day, then it is sometimes a week or so later before you see another post. The key to building your brand is consistency. I would recommend that you or someone on your team posts daily. Notice I said team! This can definitely be delegated.

However, they need to know what to post. The second error is that people post way too many educational links and stock posts that don't look unique to your practice. Remember people are on Facebook to goof off or decompress after a long day. They will not be engaged with you if all you do is post stock images.

The final error that I see is that people fail to understand the magnitude of Facebook to get their ads to their ideal audience. For example, if you want your post to be seen by mothers of kids who are between the ages of 8-16 who attend a particular school in your town, you can do so.

Sometimes you may hear dentists say, "Oh, Facebook doesn't work, or Instagram doesn't work," and so you assume those are not worth your time. But maybe it's not working because their posts are not engaging. Maybe they stopped too soon.

No matter what marketing strategy you are doing, make sure you are testing the Return on Investment (ROI). The way that you test the ROI is to ask every single patient how they heard about you then calculate how much you spent on that strategy and how much revenue was generated from those patients. You might be surprised with the results.

For example, I used to have an ad in the Yellow Pages. I tracked each month how many patients were coming in. I realized I was getting two to five patients a month. I was barely breaking even on these ads.

And then I tested my newspaper ad. I went to the local newspaper, and told them I was going to run a full color, high converting full-page ad that had been created by an award-winning graphic artist. I wanted it at the front of the publication on the right-hand side. I was very specific. I said, "If I get good results, I will continue to use this strategy."

I did get a return, but it was not worth the $800 I spent on the ad.

The only way I knew which strategies were working was to test and measure. Testing and measuring let me see that the Yellow Pages ad was ineffective, the newspaper ad wasn't producing enough of a return to justify the expense, and the social media ads were generating significant returns, up to 1,500 percent. So guess what I did? I shifted my budget to Facebook. If every time you gave me $5 I gave you $10 back, how many times would you give me $5? Figure out what is working and pour your budget into that.

The power of targeted marketing

One reason Facebook gets me excited is that it allows us to share the culture of the office and tell our story. But perhaps the most significant benefit from a marketing perspective is that you can target the exact audience that is most likely to come in and become new patients.

Social media, and specifically Facebook, has my ideal audience, 25-45 year-olds. That is an age range that is very active on Facebook. Another benefit of Facebook is that you're able to be very specific with who sees your posts in their feeds. For example, you can create posts and boost, or pay, for your posts to be seen in the newsfeeds of your current patients. You can also boost your newsfeed posts or create ads to be seen in the feeds of people who have similar preferences to your current audience, by creating a lookalike audience.

I started my journey with Facebook in 2010. I was an early adopter, and I jumped right in to take advantage of this unique opportunity never before available. At that time, most of my posts were visible in my follower's newsfeeds. However, over time, Facebook evolved and so did its algorithm.

I hear some dentists get frustrated that they now have to pay to have their posts seen by a larger audience. But what they must realize is that Facebook is a business, and a tool to help your business grow. Therefore, it is natural that you will have to pay. However, what makes Facebook unique is that you can target your posts to reach the exact people whom you intend for them to reach based on the objectives of each campaign.

You can also create marketing campaigns that are very specific to your target audience. For instance, for a back-to-school special, you can target women who have kids in a certain age who live in a particular zip code. You can also target people who are engaged in a certain age range for a teeth whitening special. Another neat feature that you can do is place a Facebook pixel on your website so that once people go to your website they can be retargeted on Facebook. This means you have specified ads (perhaps new patient specials) show up in the newsfeeds of people who have been to your website.

In addition to Facebook, we are also super active on Instagram and Twitter. We also have a presence on Google Plus and Pinterest and have just started with Snapchat.

We've made our social media marketing more efficient by using automation and scheduling where appropriate. For instance, Facebook has a tool in the private messages where you can customize your responses. You can see which questions are continuing to be asked and take the time to craft detailed responses.

You can customize the responses and then provide detailed answers to their question with a YouTube video link and a call to action. I would recommend a call to action which includes an invitation to make an online appointment.

For example, if someone asks for options for replacing missing teeth, you can click two buttons and respond to the question. This automation makes being responsive to your audience very easy and ensures consistency in responses no matter which team member is replying to the question.

Of course, social media marketing is based on

systems; therefore, in my practice, we have a team member who checks social media every hour so that we can be responsive to all of the questions and appointment requests which come in daily.

While you do have to pay for posts to be seen by a larger audience, you can get a great benefit with a small budget. My marketing budget is $500 a month. My only marketing spend is Facebook ads. And again, I've gotten a return of up to 1,500 percent. This happens when 40 new patients come in and on average spend $200. You're not going to get that type of return with any other type of marketing.

If you are just getting into Facebook advertising, focus on growing your audience and your posts.

The 7 steps to growing your first 1,000 (or next 1,000) Facebook likes

Many dentists want to know, do Facebook likes matter? Is focusing on building your Facebook community worth your time and investment? Well, after building a phenomenal dental practice that has nearly 50,000 Facebook followers and consistently getting a 1,500% ROI on Facebook, I have to say it absolutely matters!

So why are Facebook Fans so important? Well, there are several reasons. The first, and perhaps one of the most important, is that once you grow a large community of loyal fans, you increase your chances that your Facebook page will be seen. It's all about numbers! The more Fans that you have talking about you, sharing your posts and liking your content, the more your posts will go viral. Facebook allows you to build a tribe of raving fans!

By the way, building your Facebook likes will create social proof. Once people come to your page, and they see that you have thousands of Fans, they think, “Ok, this practice is doing something right.” And then they want to know more! Also, the more Fans you have, the more your posts get shared on Facebook, which helps to build your community, and ultimately your new patients.

Strategy #1: The Facebook page plugin

The Facebook page plugin lets you easily embed and promote any Facebook page on your website. Just like on Facebook, your visitors can like your Facebook page without leaving your site. Your website visitors will see a small box which includes your Facebook cover photo, a list of their friends who like your Facebook page, and a button to like your page. They also have the ability to watch the featured video attached to your Facebook page.

Here’s why you should add a Facebook Page Plugin to your website:

Visitors to your website are warm, which means they have chosen to find out more about you. This means that they are likely to follow your Facebook Page too. A Facebook Page Plugin is one of the most effective ways to grow your fan community. It is super easy to implement (takes less than 5 minutes!) and will allow first-time visitors to your site to keep in touch with what is going on in your practice.

Strategy #2: Target friends of fans with Facebook "like ads"

A very easy, inexpensive way to get more likes is by targeting friends of your current Facebook Fans. The reason this strategy works is that friends of your current Fans will likely have similar demographics to your current Fans. They live in similar communities, have similar interests, and are likely to make similar decisions when it comes to which restaurant to explore or which dentist to visit.

Here's why "like ads" work:

Like ads are the simplest to set up and are super cheap. These promotions can be boosted right from your page without having to go to the ads manager and take seconds to set up. When you attract friends of your existing Fans, you are more likely to attract a "quality" Fan.

Strategy #3: Target your existing patients

This strategy is huge! A very easy way to boost your likes, and fast, is to target your existing patients. This means that your posts get seen in the news feeds of people who already know, like, and trust you. Once you create an engaging post that talks about great things that are going on behind the scenes in your practice, they will very likely react to the post and like your page.

Here's why you should target your existing patients:

Your current patients are going to be the cheerleaders on your Facebook page, no matter if you are just getting started or when you grow thousands of Fans. They will like and share your posts, and provide social proof that your practice is the best as well as share stories with their friends of why they should become a patient of your practice.

Strategy #4: Target people who have similar characteristics to your current patients

This strategy is taking growing your fan base one step higher! Once you have created your custom audience of your existing patients, the next step is to build an audience that has similar characteristics to your current patients. You do this by creating a lookalike audience. So basically, you say "Facebook, create a list for me of people who have similar characteristics to my current patients.

Here's why you should create a look-alike audience to your current patients:

Lookalike audiences, created by Facebook, are those people who are most like your existing patients. This one is a no-brainer! This means that your posts get seen in the news feeds of people who are not current patients, but because of their likes, interests, or demographics are likely to become patients.

Strategy 5: Create a website custom audience

Website Custom Audiences (also known WCA) allow you to create Facebook ads to target people who have previously visited your website.

Why is this so amazing? Website Custom Audiences is one more way to reach an incredibly warm audience. People that have already been to your website are already exposed to your brand. Once they see your posts showing up in their feeds, they are very likely to become a fan and keep engaging with you. Website Custom Audiences allows you to target your visitors organically. Custom audiences allow you to target your patient list, but now you can reach people who may not be a patient or a current Facebook Fan, but they have visited your website.

Another very cool feature is that you can focus on those who visited a particular page or a section of your site. You can also concentrate on those who visited pages that included a particular keyword in the URL.

This customization potential for such ads is incredible.

Strategy 6: Increase your engagement

One of the most common reasons why people struggle to grow their Facebook fan base is that they don't have any engagement on their page.

If you don't have engagement, your posts won't be seen in the news feed — that is where all the action is on Facebook! You want to make sure that people are liking, reacting, commenting and sharing your content, and you must be responsive. You never want people to ask a question, and no one is there to respond.

Here's how engagement will help you attract more fans:

When you get your fans to comment and share your content, their friends will also want to jump on the bandwagon. Lots of people like to follow the crowd, and when their Facebook friends are sharing your posts, they want to know why and will want to be a part. (These shares also mean that you don't have to pay for the engagement, it just happens naturally). If you want to increase your fan base, increase your engagement!

Strategy 7: Be consistent

The final step to increasing your Fans on Facebook is to be consistent. Far too many dentists post way too infrequently to see any real results. You must create a consistent schedule for posting, and make sure that the posts are worth sharing. I recommend posting at least once daily, especially while you are growing your fan base.

Tips to help with consistency are to share the posting tasks with a member of your team using the Facebook Pages app, schedule your posts within Facebook itself, or use a scheduling automation software like Meet Edgar.

So what should you post?

If you're trying to get more likes, target creative posts to people who don't already like your page. Target people in your current community or target your custom list, which is a list — maybe a list of patients — you have uploaded. That way, they get to see the post about the charitable work and say, "Oh my gosh, my dentist is so amazing."

Create posts that are seen by people who don't follow your page. One great example is to create a post not seen in the newsfeeds of your current Fans for a new patient promotion. You could say: "50 Percent Off, Sizzling Summer Teeth Whitening Promotion! Limited Availability, Call Now" and then enter your phone number. This campaign would create more likes for your page as well as bring in new patients for teeth whitening.

You can also grow your likes by making some posts about the awesome things that you're doing in the community. The other day, we did a free dental day where we saw children who have terminal cancer. We boosted that within our actual page and had that show up in the feeds of people who currently do not like our page.

A post like that sparks an emotion in people. It indicates that your practice is different and that you're about service. When people see something like that, a company giving back, it makes them curious. We had so many likes that came from that post. People shared it. It went viral. We spent $3 to boost the post, and it got 283 likes and over 20 shares. As a result of all the shares and viral nature of Facebook, we can only imagine how many actually saw the post.

You can also use Facebook for quick promotions. For instance, let's say tomorrow falls completely apart, and you have space in your appointment book because of cancelations. Well, you can quickly pull together a promotion to get those spots filled. We have done promotions where we have offered 50 percent off cleanings for just that purpose. That's a way to fill the sudden openings you have in your schedule due to last-minute cancelations.

It's a win-win. The patient gets a great deal, and you get to fill an empty slot. Many times, those patients who come in under these special promotions end up getting additional services done or become lifelong customers.

This is why I believe in social media marketing, especially Facebook. Facebook works so well because of its targeting capabilities. It's a business strategy for growth.

Social media can be intimidating, I know. But just get started. You don't have to worry about the big numbers right off. The most important thing is to take action, and get going, so you can test and measure and find out what works for you. I would have never gotten to the point of where I have 50,000 fans if I hadn't started. When I was so early in the game, I saw people who had 1,000 likes, and I was like, "Oh my gosh, how did they get so many?"

So just get in there. Create your business page. Identify who your target market is. Look at what sort of value you can add. Decide what content is going to be most valuable. For me, it was sharing culture and talking about benefits of the services we offer. Share promotions and video testimonials. Sometimes we do little brainteasers. You want to create content people will share. When creating posts, you must always ask yourself will this post create a like, share, or click? If not, rework the post.

Once you start creating engaging content, then the next step is to create strategies for people to see that content you are creating. This is where your marketing budget comes in. Facebook ads are a phenomenal way to grow your community. You can start small. I started with $50 a month because I was trying to test and measure. Begin with a $50 budget, a $30 budget. Test and see what works for you. Once you see you are getting a return, then the next step is to increase your budget. I used to have a Yellow Pages ad. I pulled the money I used to put into Yellow Pages and put it into Facebook when the Yellow Pages contract was up.

One last point I'd like to make about social media, before moving on, is this: Social media is immediate, and it is powerful. It's fascinating and exciting because what often happens is that so many patients come in, and we ask, "How did you hear about us?" And they say, "Facebook."

Then they have a story to tell. One lady shared, "All my friends were saying they liked your page. I was determined I was not going to like your page, but finally, something showed up in my newsfeed, and I just had to like your page. I came into the office, and everything they were saying is so true. I'm Wowed."

Another lady said, "I came to this office because I kept seeing all these testimonials from all these people saying they were Wowed. I thought it was a gimmick. But there was tea! There were plantain tarts! I inspected the bathroom. There were toothbrushes! Then I sat down and waited, and the massage came. I put on the headphones. It really is what you say it is."

Your patients' story may be the most important thing for building a trusting relationship with them. Take the time to listen to your patients. Ask them how they heard about your practice. So when patients come in from social media, we say, "Tell us your story." They've seen us on Facebook. They've been to our website. They say, "Your website is amazing. I see the life-changing work you do. I want you to do it for me."

It's like word-of-mouth, but it's word-of-mouth on steroids. They're ready. They see me as an expert, and I've never met them before. And that is thanks to what we are doing on social media. We are showing who we are, even before they get to the office.

Social media lets you create this sort of virtual community. It's so awesome. Having this social media adds that credibility. People come in and they trust me. They know I'm a humble person. They know I give back to a different charity every month. They know we have quality and consistency. They have seen the testimonials.

There are so many people who know they need to go to the dentist. They know they have a problem. They don't know where to go. So when I am targeting people on Facebook, I'm not targeting people who have a dentist. If they have a dentist and are happy, that's fine. I'm targeting people who don't have a dentist or who have a need and are scared and haven't been in a few years. They come in and it's a really cool connection, and it's possible because of social media.

If you want to know where to start, visit our page at http://facebook.com/jamaicasmiles for creative ideas! Also, make sure to investigate the pages of other dentists in your community, around the country and the world and make a list of which posts are getting likes, shares, and clicks. Do your research!

A game-changer for me when I started my social media journey was using a content creation company. I was an early client of My Social Practice, which was founded in 2009. They gave me great ideas of trending dental topics, with graphics to post on Facebook. I also started to integrate posts showing the culture of my practice, as well as started to dive deep into mastering the targeting capabilities of Facebook ads, which is what quickly grew my fan base and engagement.

An excellent book that I would recommend you read is Likeable Social Media by Dave Kerpen. This book was another game-changer for me when I began my social media journey. (Dave later went on to found Likeable Dentists, a media company which helps dentists manage their social media.)

Different social networks provide different benefits. So while Facebook has the excellent targeting capabilities, we use Google Plus for search engine optimization (SEO).

Our YouTube channel is pretty dynamic. We share the community service we do, patient testimonials, as well as educational content. We have sectioned it out into the different services we provide, such as crowns, after-treatment instructions, etc. Video is huge! And remember that YouTube is owned by Google, so you definitely want a presence there as well.

The little-known secret to building a fascinating brand

Are you ready to skyrocket your brand? I mean take it to a whole different dimension? I will share with you the one thing that has catapulted my happiness and my brand. This one thing has connected me to more people and allowed people in my community to view my practice in a whole new way.

It's not the on-time guarantee; it's not the perfume in the bathroom. It's not even the dentistry. The one thing that has set us apart in our community is our serious commitment to charity. In fact, our #1 focus for this year is on our community impact. If you choose to focus on building stronger communities, you will quickly become a community leader and distinguish your brand.

By supporting people in need, you not only help the community, but you also help yourself. In our case, we support a different charity each month. Service has always been close to my heart, as I have been volunteering and supporting causes since high school. Paying it forward and making a difference in the lives of others can only lead to happiness, and I have experienced that the more that I give, the more I receive. Giving back through my business, where I can support some of the community's neediest residents, involves the team and allows us to change lives.

A few years ago we created Project Smile, our free smile makeover competition. We used social media to promote the contest and were overwhelmed by the sheer number of entries that came into our contest email inbox. People shared a photo of their smile and shared their stories of why we should choose them. We then selected three finalists, who came into the office to get a complimentary cleaning, exam and X-rays, and then we selected a final winner. The year 2013 was a particularly challenging year for us to choose a winner. One entrant was a teacher on a very fixed income. She was missing her lower front teeth and was extremely embarrassed because her students were always questioning her about why her smile "looked like that." The other finalist was a lady who was literally begging and crying because her self-esteem was low. She opened her mouth and showed her missing front tooth. The last finalist was a high school student who was born with cleft palate. He came in with his mother, and they were both excited that he might get the opportunity to finally "look normal."

We were so touched by the three applicants that we chose all three. Genuine tears of happiness and joy were had by all at the completion of their treatment. Giving back, through my gift of dentistry, as well as choosing all three candidates, was one of the best decisions that I ever made in my career as a dentist. In making a choice to give, people in the community took notice of us, and we started to receive.

If you are like me, there is some likelihood that you became a dentist because you have a strong desire to help others. Well, in the stressed out, overworked environment many of us find ourselves in, we soon forget why we got into this profession. Well, I encourage you to find a way to get back to this. You don't have to do what I do, and support a different charity each month, but do something.

There are so many ways we can all help and do charity in the world. Find a way that is close to your heart and do it. Having a dental practice that is involved in charity helps you Wow customers and your community, and makes your practice unique.

While giving back makes you feel good on the inside and helps those you are serving, it also has the added benefit of growing your brand.

Host/beneficiary arrangements provide credibility to your brand and a boost to your marketing

Many dentists think you need to spend a lot on marketing. In fact, I hear so many dentists and entrepreneurs in general say that you have to spend money to make money. However, there are some times when that rule does not apply. And honestly, these are the rules that I want to play by. This one strategy that I will lay out for you has allowed me to build partnerships with top companies in my community, reach out to my ideal patients, and become 28 percent more profitable. This one marketing strategy that I discovered a while back that has helped me to boost my brand is the Host/Beneficiary arrangement.

The Host/Beneficiary arrangement is an advanced marketing strategy where your company teams up with a more established or bigger business in your area that serves an audience that is similar to your own.

The basic way it works is this: You offer a free or deeply discounted offer to customers of the larger organization. The larger organization (the host) shares this offer with its customers. You (the beneficiary) get the implied endorsement of the host.

In the business world how this works is that you research companies in your area that have customers who would also be ideal customers to your business. You approach the company and create a great free (or discounted) offer that you would like for them to share with clients.

If the company likes your quality and finds the

offer useful, there is a good chance it will agree to the arrangement. So why would this bigger company agree to promote your business? Because it's a no-cost way to provide something of value to its customers. The host company doesn't have to pay for the perk you give. You offer it at no cost to the organization.

I decided to apply this advanced strategy to my dental practice, and instead of offering a perk or promotion to its customers, I offered it to their teams.

This is how it looked in my practice: We created an email that included an offer of 50 percent off dental cleanings and shared it with the biggest bank in the country. The email stated that because we both believe in building communities and building strong teams, we have decided to create this partnership. The employees were free to use their insurance and share the offer with their friends and family. The offer was for a limited time of one month. Well, needless to say, we were Wowed.

That month we had over 250 new patients and our revenue shot up 28 percent from the previous month. We had to hire an additional hygienist because of the rapid growth!

We attribute the success of this campaign to the great offer as well as to the fact that the team's company shared it. Incidentally, even though we offered a promotional price, more than 50 percent of the patients added on additional same-day services such as adult sealants, fluoride, and fillings, and scheduled for future treatment.

Because of our culture of Delivering WOW, after receiving unexpected bonuses such as a complimentary arm and hand massage, a full office tour, and an iPad and headphones to take away the sound, they became raving fans.

Because of the success of this campaign, we now create host/beneficiaries for cleanings with one large and one small company every month. We also offer it to the team of the charity that we are supporting that month.

So perhaps your next question is, "How do I set up these host/beneficiaries?" Well, sometimes it's all about the relationships. The easiest way to "get through" is to ask a patient who works at the company to make the connection.

Or you can "cold call," but you might not get 100 percent agreeing to the partnership. However, even if the acceptance rate is 20 percent, that is quite fine as there are limitless options of companies that can be contacted. I would suggest making the offer for them to share with their team vs. their customers, as they will look like a winner to their employees.

And remember, this is a task that can be delegated.

This strategy speaks to what a new patient is worth. You see, it didn't cost more than an email to create and market the campaign. It cost us a little chair time and some prophy paste. But the value of that campaign will last a lifetime!

Have you been at the supermarket or the mall and someone asked you what you do, and you tell them that you are a dentist? Then they start pouring out stories of the problems that they have with their teeth and what needs to be done. Then they say that they wish they could go to the dentist, but they don't have any insurance.

They might even ask you for a discount.

What they are really saying is "How can I afford dental care? Show me how I can afford dental care."

Well, host/beneficiary arrangements can help here as I share in the story below.

In fact, you can get some of your best patients when you meet people in a restaurant, at your kid's school, or even in a parking lot. They want to know how you can make it easy for them to receive treatment.

Recently, I was at a leading hardware store, and the topic came up that I was a dentist. The man asked if I could give him a "discount." I told him that I could do something for his entire company. I said I could make a special offer for them all to come in for cleanings for the next month for 50 percent off!"

"Wow, you would do that?" he asked. "Of course." I then asked him to provide me with the details of the person at the hardware store who could share the offer with the team, and he did just that.

Offering a special promotion for his company was an excellent way for me to get in front of ALL of the employees of the company, and help him out at the same time.

Now, getting these patients in for the first visit is just the first step. You want to make sure that you have a system in place to offer extended payment plans with a third party so that if they need extended treatment over time, they will be able to take advantage of flexible monthly payments.

For procedures over a certain dollar amount, you could also offer a 5% pre-payment courtesy if they schedule that month and an additional 5% if they pre-pay for their treatment. (Of course, this takes into account that you have set your fees accordingly to accommodate everyone taking advantage of this offer.)

Strategic alliances help grow your reach

Another great way to build your brand and grow your practice is through strategic alliances. Strategic alliances allow you to gain access to people and resources you may not otherwise be able to access.

In a strategic alliance, you team up with another business or organization to do a project or certain initiative together. You agree to share resources so you can both gain access to whatever resources you feel you cannot get alone.

For instance, you might develop a strategic alliance with a bridal shop. You might offer a 50 percent discount on teeth whitening to all brides who schedule an appointment and mention the postcard or flyer they got from the bridal shop. The bridal shop gets to offer brides a substantially discounted gift in the form of teeth whitening. You get the opportunity to land a new customer. The bride gets the chance to put on her best smile for her special day.

Teaming up in this way with a bridal shop is a perfect fit for your dental practice, as brides are often in the market for cosmetic dentistry.

Another alliance that we set up was with a top local sushi restaurant. They designed an electronic coupon for a free dessert for our patients to receive during their birthday month. We include this “gift” to our patients with the auto responder that goes out to our patients on their birthdays. It is a win-win-win. Our patients get a gift; the restaurant gets more customers, and we can add value to our patients without paying a thing.

You can get creative when considering strategic alliances. Look at what you can provide to the other side, and what you expect to receive. It's important that both sides are receiving value; otherwise, the alliance will not work.

A strategic alliance can help you to grow your practice in a significant way, as you gain new customers, resources, and other benefits of joining forces with another organization.

Delivering WOW creates raving fans

Once you have your Wow culture in place and the systems to ensure that there is consistency, then you are well on your way to creating your fascinating brand.

When your patients are Wowed, whether by the amazing dentistry that you provide or how you make them feel, they will want to tell the world. I'm sure you've been a raving fan of another company at some point or another. What is that one thing that they did to captivate you? This feeling of captivation with your practice is what you want your patients to feel.

When you deliver on your promise of Wow, you will find that patients will be so thrilled that they want the people who matter most to them to experience the same joy.

So get all the other Delivering WOW elements in order, use these marketing strategies to turbo charge your promotional efforts, and be prepared to ignite!

Be sure to do what we discussed in chapter 8, and that is to listen to understand. Listen to what your patients are saying and what they want. Why are they choosing you? Remember that all the work of Delivering WOW is not about you; it's about your patient. Provide tremendous value and you'll get massive results.

People buy what they want, not what they need. So find out what your patients want, and then give it to them!

Some spend thousands on ineffective marketing, such as Yellow Pages ads that no longer work. You don't want to do that. Test and measure your marketing efforts, so you know what actually works for you.

Make sure to keep in regular contact with your patients through monthly newsletters and promotions. And be sure that your website is current and has opt-ins for you to follow up with prospective customers as well as a Facebook pixel so that your practice will stay at the top of their minds. This way Wow isn't a one-time event, but an ongoing activity.

DELIVERING WOW ACTION ACTIVITY

Evaluate your brand. What does your brand say when you are not around? Is it fascinating? Ask your team, you friends, and your patients how they would describe your brand. Look at the responses. Is it aligned with your brand story, if not create a list of what you can do to make that change.

CHAPTER 10

Ignite your passion

Now imagine your new life, your new practice, one with purpose. One where you can choose the lifestyle you wish to live. When you live your purpose, you wake up every day and say, "Wow, I am changing the world!" Make sure to know your purpose. If you don't know what your life's purpose is and how your business can amplify it, that's totally OK. If you don't know your purpose, then your purpose is to find your purpose. It took me a while to come to my purpose, which is to leave a positive impact on everyone that I come in contact with, including my family, my patients, my community, and dentists.

What's your purpose? You might find an answer very quickly, and then you decide no, that's not it. Then you try again. This is a process that you have to develop. But keep asking yourself, and one day you will find that purpose which will be so compelling that it speaks for itself.

Next, find those around you who resonate with you finding that purpose. Once you know your purpose and those who you want to serve with that purpose, start learning from them. Ask them, and they'll guide you to more success and more wealth.

We recently had a return visit from a patient who first came in two months ago. On her first visit, she shared that she was truly petrified of going to the dentist and told us she might even bite! We just smiled because we knew that she, just like so many other fearful patients, would be transformed. We would Wow her, and her fear would melt away. We told her that at the end of the appointment, she would be so relaxed that she would want not to bite, but to give a hug. We were confident.

We worked with her, on easing her anxiety and were confident that she would get the result she desired. We relaxed her with soothing music and the complimentary massage; we took the time to allow her to express her fears. We listened to understand. We provided solutions to her problems and did not judge. Now, things have completely turned around for her. She is no longer petrified. And she has been able to undergo the necessary procedures. In fact, we've now gotten her to a place where she has completed all of her work. Upon her follow-up visit, she said, "Doc, this place is truly amazing."

The essence of the Wow experience is individual care of individual patients each and every time. That is the highest level of customer service. I could not have done that by myself. Getting a win like this goes back to the culture of the place. One of our core values is to deliver a Wow experience every time. That is important to us, and it comes across in how we treat each patient.

We have those wins every single day. When you implement the changes I've discussed in this book and master the Delivering WOW areas I've outlined, you will transform your business. Period. In fact, you, and your practice will be respected in the community, and you will have raving fans. You will have team members who love working in your practice, and you will finally get to enjoy your business, and your life more.

Remember that story I shared at the beginning of the book, the story of Dr. Scott, the anxious, stressed, and overwhelmed dentist who had no time to attend her child's sporting events and was fighting with her husband over how much time she was spending at work? Her health was taking a beating as her blood pressure was going up and her work was no longer enjoyable.

Well, that story has changed, after committing to becoming a Delivering WOW practice. Dr. Scott now is again finding joy in her work. She is working less but bringing in more revenue. She now has time for all the activities that are important to her — including attending her son's ball games, working out, and spending quiet time with her husband. Her marriage is no longer filled with fights and discord. She is off her blood pressure medication and is planning her big vacation to a dream destination for the next quarter.

So what happened? Delivering WOW happened.

While this is a story I created to illustrate the experiences of so many burned out and stressed out dentists, the outcome you can experience is real. When you put in place the right systems and team, and get the branding down and exemplify the core values and culture that are attractive to your ideal customer, you truly can have a breakthrough. You can have a practice that fulfills your vision and gives you more joy. You can find that you have more time to experience life, more money to give you the freedom you desire, and improved relationships, health, and quality of life.

That is the power of Delivering WOW.

You can change the future of your practice and your life. You can design your future. Business doesn't have to take over your life. You, through your practice, can make a positive contribution to the community. Your practice can have a brand that sets it apart. Struggle can finally be a thing of the past.

You can have patients who love coming to see you,

and when they leave, they say, “This was the best dental experience of my life!”

This can be your new Wow reality.

DELIVERING WOW ACTION ACTIVITY

Write down what you have learned about Delivering WOW and how you can apply it to your practice.

CHAPTER 11

Going forward

Purpose, passion, and persistence. These make up the secret sauce to success. Dentistry is not about fixing or repairing teeth. It's about the end benefits of what solutions you are providing. It's about changing lives.

The best dentists realize that what's most important is the end benefit. You are giving someone confidence to go after that new job. You are giving someone better health because their gums won't get a disease. You are giving someone longevity in life. You are giving someone a job, so they can now achieve their life's passion. When you discover this, then creating a fascinating practice will be easy.

My goal in writing this book is to inspire dentists along their journey to think out of the box. You don't have to accept the status quo as an unshakeable reality. You don't have to feel stuck in your practice, stressed out, and receiving no real joy. No, you can create a Wow practice and have an extraordinary business with massive growth.

You've got the plan. Now, it's up to you. What will you do now? Will you continue in the same way, or will you take what you've learned here and get going on creating Wow in your business? And there is no need to be scared or intimidated that it's too late for you: It doesn't matter how long you've been in business because Delivering WOW isn't about where you start. It's about where you can finish.

You don't have to continue slogging away, thinking it will take you 20 years or more to get to a good place. You can get to a Wow place now. Growing your business isn't about what you do someday. It's about what you choose to do, starting today.

I invite you to be a part of the Delivering WOW experience. Start now by taking your practice and your life to the next level. I've pointed you in the direction, but this book is just the start. You will have more to learn to dive deeper. If you know you want to, for example, master today's top marketing strategy of social media, then commit to a course. Get a coach. Join a mastermind or an online community of like-minded dentists who will stretch you and hold you accountable.

I continue to learn, and my mastermind partners help to keep me focused. Your vision, too, will involve many others. Be prepared to get them excited and engaged to take the journey with you.

It's all about action

One caution, though, as you go forward: Learning is great. Wonderful. But the transformation you seek will not happen without action. So don't just read what I've written. Act upon it. Anything you want to improve is something you need to focus on. If you want to have more profits in your business, you need to focus on all steps that make up profits. If you want to work fewer days a week, then put the steps in place to make that happen. If you want to take a trip, book the ticket.

If your aim is to create a Wow dental practice, then write down what you want, put in place the steps, and take action! Remember:

Write the vision. Be specific. Engage others in your vision, and get them excited about supporting it.

Identify your culture. Determine the type of company culture you need that will help you move toward your vision. What story will you tell the world about your practice?

Focus on the set of core values that set the tone around the practice. Live your core values and make them the heart of your practice.

Hire and train the right team. Invest in your team's professional development and learning. Be open to your team, listen to them, and encourage them to see themselves in your vision. Delegate, automate, or eliminate tasks that take you away from doing what you do best in your business.

Implement systems for the repeatable activities you engage in. Write down all of the steps for every process in your practice, and review twice a year to ensure that all stays current.

Share your brand through strategic marketing so you attract your ideal customers. Put in place social media marketing, as well as implement some of the other marketing strategies discussed in the book. Always test and measure.

Listen to my Delivering WOW Dental Podcast on iTunes. Join my free Facebook Group at www.deliveringwowhangout.com. Visit my website at www.deliveringwow.com for free resources and reports to help you scale up and get massive results.

You are now equipped to take a giant step forward.

Think Big and Have Fun.

Now GO and start Delivering WOW!

ABOUT THE AUTHOR

Dr. Anissa Holmes has been voted one of the Top 25 Women in Dentistry by Dental Products Report, and has the leading dental practice for Delivering WOW in Jamaica.

A social media strategist, author, speaker, podcaster, and practicing dentist, she shows dentists how to create profitable and thriving businesses.

She is a graduate of the University of Alabama School of Dentistry and lives in Jamaica with her husband and two children.

She loves to hear from readers.

Connect with her in the following ways:

• Join the free Delivering WOW Facebook group at: www.deliveringwowhangout.com

• Visit her website at http://deliveringwow.com

• Like her Facebook page at http://facebook.com/jamaicasmiles

• Subscribe to her Delivering Wow Dental Podcast on iTunes at https://itunes.apple.com/us/podcast/delivering-wow-dental-podcast/id1072610113

Made in the USA
Middletown, DE
10 July 2017